Never at This Level

Far from the MCC
1998-2017

by
Ian Howarth
Antony Mann
Mike Reeves

with
Stuart Ackland
Matt Bullock
Derek Hambridge
James Hoskins
Gareth Timms
Jan Webster

photography
James Hoskins
Ian Howarth

and contributions from
Jake Hotson
Ben Mander

First published in Great Britain in 2018

Printed by Fine Print Services Ltd
Witney
Oxfordshire
fineprint.co.uk

(for which the club is indebted to Russell Turner)

ISBN 978-1-78808-353-9

Back Row (seated): Jon Newman, Mike Reeves, Matt Bullock, Geoff Carter, Mark Rundle, Gary Timms
Middle Row (from Giant Duck): James Hoskins, Chris Williams, Dave Shorten Andrew Darley, Lee Ainsworth
Front Row: Jake Hotson, James Pearson, Martin Westmoreland, Ian Howarth, Russ Turner

NEVER AT THIS LEVEL

All around me are familiar pitches
Worn out wickets, worn out tickets
Bright and early for an opening batsman
Getting no runs, getting no runs
Their tears are filling up their average
No expression, no direction
Hide my head I want to kill the umpire
Nothing shiny, nothing tiny
And I find it kind of funny
I find it kind of sad
The dreams in which I'm scoring
Are the best I've ever had
I find it hard to pick you
I find it hard to sweep
When people run in singles
It's a very, very
MAD world

Bowlers waiting for the day they feel good
5-for nineteen, get a hat-trick
And I feel the way of every 'keeper
Catch and stump 'em, catch and stump 'em
Went to bowl and I was very nervous
No line no length, no line no length
Hello skipper tell me what's my action
Bowl right through me, bowl into me
And I find it kind of funny
I find it kind of sad
The dreams in which I'm striking
Are the best I've ever had
I find it hard to york you
I find it hard to spin
When people guard their leg stump
It's a very, very
MAD world
MAD world
Enlarging your world
MAD world

Andrew Morley
with apologies to R J Orzabel de la Quintana

NEVER AT THIS LEVEL

Foreword

IT is now 20 years since the club was founded by that inspiration and wise polymath Noel Reilly, bon viveur, publican, former soldier, artist (in every sense) and poet. A generous host, kindly and friendly, the ideal Jericho landlord at "The Jude the Obscure". Noel had a brilliant idea (with the help of sometime bar associates Ed Lester and Ruth) of forming a cricket team, from many of his diverse customers and as such an interesting mix pot Pouri, of individuals, characters, varying from professional musicians to tree surgeons and the odd gynaecologist.

If you were, vulnerable, in need of help, support, and above all friendship, then it was more likely that you would be asked by Noel; who you were or what you were was of no consequence to be invited to participate. In some ways, it was almost as if Noel was selecting for a therapeutic regime rather than a cricket team.

It is a testament to those involved in running the team over the intervening 20 years that despite many transitions of grounds, watering holes and landlords, which would have stopped other better funded or more prestigious organisations, this cricket team has survived and prospered. Of the cricketers; there have been many and diverse, "never mind the quality – feel the width", players in essence have been of the same model, a few have been there too most of the time, and essentially at any point in time there have been four or five stalwarts each providing various functions, such as organising the fixtures, picking the team, organising the annual cricket tour, the stats, including fantasy cricket based on the team players' own performances, in teams, about themselves picked by themselves.

A tradition that started from initial days; of writing match reports to a high literary standard, sometimes themed, generally in an amusing and supportive tone. The first of these being the great Australian author and fast bowler Antony Mann. These match reports provide enjoyable and interesting reading. Along with the written record of match report articles, has evolved a contemporaneous tradition of highly professional match and tour photography.

So, enjoy this book produced to celebrate the 20th anniversary of the founding of this important development in world cricketing culture.

Tony Mander FRCOG (Doc)
January 2018

NEVER AT THIS LEVEL

IGNOBLE STRIFE AND WHY I LOVE IT

Jan Webster
Player #123

IGNOBLE STRIFE

JUST like Somerset and Northamptonshire CCCs, the Far from the MCC have never won the County Cricket championship. Unlike those counties, however, this doesn't seem to gnaw away at the soul of the club. *'The thoughtless world to majesty may bow [and] exalt the brave, & idolize success'*, as Thomas Gray once put it, but it requires a very different kind of collective idiot joy to be able, say, to celebrate a man falling into a hedge as the team highlight of a very long afternoon spent playing cricket in the shadows of what looks like the Arkham Asylum from the Batman movies as this club did relatively recently.

It's not clear whether Gray was a cricket fan, but since half his poem, *Elegy Written in an Country Churchyard,* has him musing over the graves of his contemporaries, it suggests someone well able to find comfort, pleasure even, in the ultimate failure of his fellow men. This essential schadenfreude rather brings us to this particular cricket club, and what I love about it – what Gray called *Far from the Madding CC's 'ignoble strife '*.

Cricket clubs are funny things. It's easy enough to find one (I've seen a concrete cricket pitch in Minsk and watched a game or two in Vancouver, even Carterton has a ground, I believe), but it's finding the right one that that's tricky. Some clubs advertise, The MAD's process seems similar to a carpet roller picking up lint. My own experience with the MAD was a simple matter of ineluctable fate – although Mr Ian Howarth once kindly remarked, "What other shithouse team would have you?" which has a certain harsh ring of truth to it.

League cricket finally lost its appeal for me one damp Saturday night in June in Glasgow in 2009. It was a quarter to ten at night and both teams were still grinding our way to a stupendously boring draw after 90 overs of near inertia. I couldn't feel my fingers, the opposition, frankly, were the kind you'd cross a road to avoid, and the whole affair just felt like a chore; everything seemed predicated on the few measly points available at the end of the game. We sometimes seemed to travel miles for some games to turn out against teams determined to ape all the shoddier elements of professional sport (largely a matter of overpriced equipment and being arseholes). It all seemed to be too *serious* and lacking something really basic. This was supposed to be my leisure time, my *fun* time, and sometimes fun felt that it was at a premium. How serious does cricket have to be?

The Joker is housed top left apartment

In 2011 we moved back south, back to Oxford and one wet afternoon we pottered over to Wantage. The town, largely famous for King Alfred and shoddy cake management, also has a proper bookshop, one of a dying breed, called The Regent. Once there I gravitated towards the sports section to see what sort of cricket book selection there was and found what they used to call a 'slim volume' entitled '*Not At This Level*'. It detailed the first ten years of existence of a pub team which no longer had a pub. The sheer detail and effort crammed into this little book seemed to demonstrate a dangerous level of obsession, leavened mainly by a certain black humour and a tendency towards benign lunacy. A team so unhinged that they actually wrote a book about it seemed… quite a good thing actually. It suggested a certain amount of pride and of continuity.

The Aussies have a term for a particular type of cricket fan; a 'tragic'. I reckon I am one, up to a point at least. I'm immoderately fond of the game and all its peripheral faff (all those ticking stats and stories, love 'em), but as my wisdom and competence ebb and flow in exact proportion I'm less and less bothered about the result and far more interested in having an interesting time. Essentially, I like playing cricket, watching cricket, and talking about cricket. I also like talking bollocks about anything else in good company and drinking beer, preferably in nice fields.

As luck would have it my new works team had some pre-season nets in Cowley and we were forced to share the sports hall with what looked at first glance like some kind of care in the community project. No one ever looks at their best in the nets or on Sunday mornings, but this lot was like watching a deformed and almost satanic simulacrum of cricket through a lysergic kaleidoscope; a distorted and writhing orgy of sweat, swearing, cross bats and bowling actions which appeared to be based on hammer throwing. At least they were friendly though, welcoming even. And they appeared to quite like each other, *and* they looked like they were *enjoying* themselves. Most odd. Dimly, I realised the man they called Moo looked familiar from somewhere. Of course! It was the man on the front cover of *Not at This Level.* I had found The MAD.

In May of 2012 I made my debut against Milton CC. We arrived in a green field, a very green field. It was pleasant enough, but it seemed to lack a cricket pitch, or at least did until the oppo arrived and made one seconds before the game started. It was a blazing hot day and the game set a pattern which has since become very familiar to me. We drank beer before the game, we went from 77-2 to 84-6, then managed to go from 106-6 to 110 all out to lose. Mike Reeves scored 30 odd and took a couple of wickets, then we went to a pub and moaned a bit. It was bloody ace.

Me, playing a delightful shot off the fearsome pie of Keith Ponsford.

A key hint to the nature of this club is to be found on home page of the website: 'Far from the MCC' it headlines, and underneath that it also says, 'a friendly Oxford cricket team'. Pleasingly, this is actually a perfectly accurate description of The MAD. 'Friendly' is actually something absolutely fundamental to the club, not just in the way the team plays, but also in the way it socialises – it's even enshrined in the club's constitution. It's nice to be nice they say, and, generally, other teams like playing The MAD. They know they'll get a decent game played as it should be. As part of this the club is good at welcoming new players and also partners. I've played for clubs where the presence of a partner is treated with the kind of suspicion usually reserved for shoplifters.

The MAD is also a club where pleasure is taken in a far broader array of ideas than simply that of runs scored and wickets taken. Meeting in new pubs before

Me, with some of the guys high-fiving my head

the game is part of it, the chance to play on some lovely grounds is another. Andy Darley pirouetting round his wicket before hitting them with his own testicles is a fairly typical cherished moment. This means there is actually a rich and sophisticated depth to what might look to a casual observer to be some kind of cricketing adult crèche. So, this is clearly not a club which revolves entirely about the relative skills of a player. A great batsman or bowler who was a match winner, but who was also a bell end would not last long at The MAD. There is almost as much pride in the scores against the team (Hyron Shallow, Jay Rahman!) or the most ducks and run outs as the feats performed by our own players. There is room for both 'good' and 'bad' cricket in this club, provided it is done with good humour and positive intent. "PMA!" (or positive mental attitude) is a cry which occasionally goes around, largely from James Hoskins, who, to be fair, genuinely seems to follow the doctrine whereas for most it seems tinged with a certain irony. The sight of Spam or Dave Emerson charging down the wicket to the first ball of a 40 over game regardless of the ball's trajectory or likely outcome is a typical MAD sight, as is Dave Shorten suggesting we can 'turn this round' after the oppo have scored 150 off the first 15 overs. No one actively enjoys a pasting, but I've never seen The MAD leave a game with their heads down. About the only thing which seems to wind the club up is another team not playing in the right spirit and this is usually resolved by some judicious editing of the fixture list.

This is also not a club that plays cricket as if the game itself is not worth taking seriously. In the end, it doesn't *really* matter, but, it has to matter *in the moment* or there is no point playing. The MAD manage to balance these two apparently conflicting notions without stress and largely because it attracts people who can understand this without having to articulate it.

As with any club, the credit goes to those who put the time in to make this happen and who ensure that the spirit of the club is maintained. While pretty much every one of the 145 players who have turned out for The MAD since 1998 has contributed to some degree or another, since I've been playing the likes of Spam, Moo, Timms, Reevsie, Matt, Russ, JMO, Dave have skippered, organised, cursed and guided the club onwards in a way that's managed to maintain a sense of serious cricketing fun. They have shepherded this friendly, mildly obsessive Oxford cricket team into its third decade

Chapeau to the Board and up The MAD. Here's to the next 10 or 20 or… ■

Jan Webster

Geoff – waiting for the talent that never comes

Contents: Part 1

Misremembered Days Remembered
Far from the MCC 1998-2007

Antony Mann

AS I write this at the fag end of 2017, Australia are 3-0 up in the Ashes, but Alastair Cook is 244 not out in the 4th Test at Melbourne, so the veteran English opener has at last put some runs on the board. Not when it mattered though, eh Cookie? Couldn't have done it when the series was still in the balance, could you? Anybody can hit a quick double ton when the pressure is off or when they are badly hung over, as Ian Howarth will tell you. Cook, you are a joke.

Today, 2017 seems a long time from 2007, or ten years, whichever is the longer. It was in 2007 that *Far From the MCC*'s first book, *Not at This Level*, was compiled. That book contained a history of *Far from the MCC*, called *Misremembered Days*. It was about a bunch of people that nobody had ever heard of, and their exploits and adventures on the green and pleasant cricket grounds in and around Oxford, and that rank mud bowl up at Kidlington.

It's hard to remember now much about the writing of *Misremembered Days*, which seems appropriate. Why do we remember things in the first place? Is it because if we don't, we'll never know what we were going to buy for dinner, or is there some deeper reason? Say what you like about shopping, it always works better when you have a list. If you don't, then you are bound to forget the most important ingredient, usually beer. The same is true for histories of cricket clubs. Unless everything is recorded at the time it happens, when it comes to writing the history of something, for instance, *Far from the MCC*, there are bound to be errors, some intentional, some not.

The chronicles of *Far from the MCC* are incomplete, at least with regard to the early days. Due to the primitive technology of the late 1990s, coupled with complete indifference, there are large gaps in the history, but thankfully that was never an obstacle to this historian, since a lot of *Misremembered Days* was completely fabricated.

Misremembered Days Remembered is a shorter version of *Misremembered Days*, and also riddled with inaccuracies. And yet, like the work it is drawn from, it remains completely true.

Where it all started some many years after it all started

1997

On New Year's Eve, 1997, at the Jude the Obscure pub in Walton Street, Oxford, *Jude the Obscure CC* is formed at the instigation of local enthusiast Eddie Lester. The landlord of the pub, Noel Reilly, is the club's patron and throws in 100 quid for bats, pads and gloves. Nobody thinks anything will come of it, this crazy idea of forming a cricket team, and the next day, everyone has forgotten about it. Except for one person. Eddie.

1998

The first captain of Jude the Obscure CC is Eddie Lester, or possibly Fred Townsend. Nobody knows for sure. Nobody cares.

The first game is played against Research Machines, a loss by 118 runs. Matt Bullock, Howard Jones, Antony Mann and Lee Davie all play for *The Jude* in 1998. Of that first season's players, only Matt Bullock remains at the club, and has been the Chairman ever since.

1998-2007

Playing at Cuttleslowe Park one Sunday afternoon, meningeal fluid leaks from the nose of James Blann while he is taking a spectacular catch. Meningeal fluid is the stuff in your head which keeps your brain in a nice bath of comforting liquid. We never find out what becomes of James. But at least we all know what meningeal fluid looks like. For the record, it's runny and white.

1999

The Jude is now an established local club, lacking in skill but filled with enthusiasm for the noblest sport of all. Drinking. They also like cricket, and led by its first actual captain, Eddie Lester, the team aspires to leave utter ineptitude behind and attain the Holy Grail of mediocrity.

In fact, some members of *The Jude* toy with the idea of becoming a Saturday league team, but soon abandon the plan. There are too many dickheads in league cricket, not to mention league cricketers can actually play.

Committing themselves to Sundays, *The Jude* play their home games on local council pitches like Cuttleslowe and Cowley Marshes, and travel away to picturesque village grounds where the pub is always right across the road and the tea is more than just a bag of cheese and onion crisps from the Co-op.

Early days in The Jude

Beating proper established cricket sides is still too much for *The Jude*, although they do defeat *The Marlborough House* thanks to a nice 68 from Lee Davie. Marlborough player Mike Reeves scores 102 not out in the loss, the first of many times *The Jude* will charitably facilitate an opposition player's scoring of their first (and only) century.

Chris Legg and Mike Thorburn are regular players, and 1999 also sees the debut of Ben Mander and his eminent gynaecologist father Tony.

Also new to the club this year is James Hoskins, who lives just down the road from Cuttleslowe Park. Hoskins turns up one day to watch *The Jude* playing a man down and by the end of the day is an integral part of the team, which he remains to this day.

2000

The Jude goes from strength to strength, and can now sometimes even put out eleven players on match day. Tellingly, as Oxford Council finally gives up the idea of supporting public cricket pitches, *The Jude* find a home pitch to play on - Pembroke Sports Ground. It is an important step for the local pub team, finding a home base where they can host visiting teams in the appropriate manner.

Clare Norris becomes a regular, an Oxford Blue with a straight bat, born two decades too early to take advantage of the remarkable rise in popularity of women's cricket. Adie Fisher signs up when his side *The Team With No Name* becomes *The Name With No Team*. Fisher is a brutal batsman who has perfected the art of pie-chucking. He will take many wickets for *The Jude* with his lobbed custard tarts and pineapple flans, all the while dispensing irrefutable cricket wisdom. *Bowlers win matches* was one of his, though no doubt he stole it from somewhere else. Fisher will also become known as one of *The Chemical Brothers*, although that is another story.

Jake Hotson plays his first game for *The Jude* at Cowley Marshes dressed in black jeans and Doc Martens, thus starting as he means to go on. Local poet and drinker (not necessarily in that order) Andrew Morley joins the side as last prize for winning the quiz at the pub one night.

This year also sees the debut of Richard Hadfield, who plays one game then goes missing in mysterious circumstances. Hadfield's whereabouts are still unknown. Has anyone seen him?

The Jude lose a lot of games in the year 2000. In fact, their only victory over decent opposition comes against *The Beehive* in the pouring rain, in their second game at Pembroke. Is this gratifying win a sign of bigger things to come? To be honest, probably not.

Noel Reilly, maverick landlord and sex magnet

2001

This year sees Eddie Lester relinquish the captaincy in favour of pro violin strummer Leo Phillips, who plays about four games for the team before buggering off to Thailand. But as players leave, so they are replaced. Nobody plays for a local pub team forever. Do they? Do they??

Howard Jones, Adie Fisher, Lee Davie, Ant Mann, Matt Bullock, the Manders, James Hoskins and Jake Hotson still make up the core of the team, and are duly joined by Steve Dobner and Thornton Smith (Chemical Brother #2). Both will become important and enduring members of *The Jude* and help shape the side's culture and ethos into what it is today. Whatever that might be. Answers on the back of an envelope.

In 2001, *The Jude*'s rivalry with *The Marlborough* is at its peak. With that season's game score at 1-1, the 'decider' between the two teams sees Jake Hotson dominate the first part of the match with best-ever figures of 5-28. The now-infamous photo of *The Jude* shows Hotson holding the 5-for ball aloft after the *Marlborough* innings, so angering the opposition that they bowl *The Jude* out for bugger all and win handily, though to be fair *The Jude* would probably have lost anyway. They still aren't very good.

2002

With Leo Phillips absconding, Matt Bullock reluctantly takes on the job of skipper. At the same time, patron and club guru Noel Reilly moves on from his long-time haunt *Jude the Obscure*, and in keeping with his penchant for naming pubs after the novels of Thomas Hardy, his new establishment in the heart of Oxford is called *Far from the Madding Crowd.*

Thus the evolution of the name and the identity of the club – to be known now as *Far from the Madding Crowd CC* – begins. No doubt if Noel had opened yet more pubs, perhaps *The Mayor of Casterbridge*, or *The Return of the Native*, the club would have adopted these names as well, though it is useless to speculate what would have happened if Reilly had ever run a place called *Tess of the D'Urbervilles.*

But it doesn't seem to matter what the team is called, winning games is still a problem. With Lee Davie and Adie Fisher missing for most of the year and no new blood to boost the paltry ranks, *The MAD* – as they are now often called, by themselves at least – manage just two wins out of eleven games for the season, the worst since the club was founded.

Even people who are used to losing eventually get sick of losing. You can only make fun of your own hopelessness for so long until it becomes self-defeating. Finding it hard to rustle up a team at the best of times, and playing poor cricket against opposition teams who are getting sick of winning so easily, in 2002 *The MAD* is in danger of going the way of most pub cricket teams – into history.

2003

But in 2003, something happens – something which alters the course of *The MAD* and assures its survival into the future. In the off season, the call goes out for new players. Not the usual bunch of hobos and indigents who have made up the team until now, but people who can actually play a bit of cricket. It is an act of faith. *The MAD* believes it can attract these players into its ranks and, lo and behold, it happens.

In 2003, a host of new players arrive from fuck knows where – Martin Westmoreland, Nick Hebbes, Steve Hebbes, John Harris and Graham Bridges. Disturbingly, some of these blokes have northern accents, but all will be forgiven if they can average more than 7 with the bat. Though Graham Bridges doesn't play for the team for long, the rest become permanent fixtures.

Under the enthusiastic captaincy of *The MAD*'s fourth skipper, James Hoskins, the team begins to win games. When Ian Howarth turns up by mistake at Cowley Marshes, thinking the ground is a pub, and plays half pissed and scores a bag of drunken runs, the transformation of *The MAD* is complete, from a bunch of no-hopers playing Sunday cricket into a bunch of competitive no-hopers playing Sunday cricket.

The MAD continue their rivalry with *The Marlborough House*, and their new nemesis is a beguiling batsman under a wide-brimmed hat who bowls like a windmill on acid. Dan Edwards plays the game hard and is never short of a chirp. He is also never out lbw, or at least should never be *given* out lbw, because the ball is always missing, or big stride, or pitching outside leg, or going over, or outside the line, or you know, not out. Not at this level. Sorry mate, you were plumb.

The MAD win seven games in 2003, and six of the first seven best batsmen are new to the team. Ian Howarth, usually drunk or hungover or both, hits 527 runs, of which he can remember none. Antony Mann takes 27 wickets at 10.52, a new record, in probably only three or four games, it's hard to be exactly certain. With new personnel and a new attitude, *The MAD* have turned a corner.

2004

In the winter of 2003, the team gather for an important cultural occasion at Noel Reilly's *Far from the Madding Crowd*. Antony Mann's book of short fiction, *Milo & I*, is launched to rapturous acclaim, and as people gather and buy more copies than they will ever need, *MAD* players get slaughtered and end the evening with an entertaining fist fight. Three of the roster end up in casualty when the booze has worn off enough that they can feel pain. It promises to be another great season.

Indeed, *The MAD* win 9 games this year, as the playing squad remains relatively unchanged. Adie Fisher is back, as are Andrew Morley and Tony Mander, but Eddie Lester is slowly extricating himself from the team he founded as he makes plans to emigrate to Middle Earth.

Back row (left to right): **Adie Fisher, Nick Hebbes, Tony Mander, Antony Mann, John Harris, Steve Dobner. Matt Bullock, Ed Lester, Thornton Smith, Mike Clarke**
Front row (left to right): **Ian Howarth, Martin Westmoreland, James Hoskins, Steve Hebbes, Jake Hotson**

New opponents *University Offices* showcase a talented all-rounder Andy Darley, while *The MAD* beat old foes *OUP* for the first time thanks to a Howarth-Hotson opening partnership of 73 of which Hotson scores 6. Adie Fisher's 5-15 in a tight victory against *The Marlborough* are career best figures and his selection of tarts, pies and flans will long be remembered.

The ugly side of village cricket is exposed as the captain of *The Baldons* is given out but stands his ground, refusing to leave the crease. After a few shabby minutes of pathetic whining and petulance, *The Baldons* skipper is permitted to resume his innings by the ever-accommodating *MAD*. The sour-faced douche goes on to score the match-winning century, no doubt his first ever, and *The MAD* have no other course left to them but to go to the pub and have a few beers. So no different from any other game.

2005

2005 is a horrendous, tragic year for cricket as, after Glenn McGrath treads on a tennis ball, Australia lose the Ashes for the first time in four hundred years. But for *The MAD*, it is yet another season of change.

The MAD finally cut their ties with Noel Reilly and are finally able to delete the third 'c' from their name. No longer *Far from the Madding Crowd Cricket Club*, they are now instead the more apt and easier to say *Far from the MCC*, and will remain so into the future. Although, without a home pub to drink in, for one year at least they will call themselves *The No-Mad.*

The addition of wicket keepers Gary Littlechild and Geoff Carter brings to eight the number of *MAD* custodians, including Matt Bullock, Ian Howarth, Steve Dobner, Adie Fisher, Thornton Smith and Lee Davie. Refugee from the floundering *Marlborough House* Dan Edwards complements existing opening batsmen Ian Howarth, Nick Hebbes, Antony Mann, Martin Westmoreland, Steve Dobner, Tony Mander, Jake Hotson, Mike Clarke James Hoskins and Lee Davie. Sadly the opening bowler department is somewhat depleted with only Antony Mann, Ian Howarth, Nick Hebbes, Martin Westmoreland, Steve Dobner and Lee Davie on the books.

John Harris takes a remarkable 7-5 against the hapless *Marlborough*, record *MAD* bowling figures which will likely never be beaten unless *The Marlborough* reform with the same batting line-up. This defeat for *The Marlborough* signals the end of the Great Rivalry which began so many years before. Like a stinking rat fleeing his sinking ship, Mike Reeves too will soon abandon his pathetic team and jump aboard *The Good Ship MAD*, joining fellow rodent escapee Dan Edwards.

2005 also sees the debut of Ian Howarth's better half Vicki Stone, whose duck epitomises her deep and abiding indifference to cricket in all its forms.

2006

This year *The MAD* take up residence at *The Magdalen Arms* on the Iffley Road. Somehow convincing the landlord that every Sunday they will fill the pub with hundreds of cricketers and their fawning groupies scores them a cool 500 quid for the coffers. To be fair, the half dozen players who do turn up after each game and stay for one beer don't much like the pub anyway.

As James Hoskins sets down the sceptre of captaincy after three years of being hassled by people for a bowl or a bat, it is Ian Howarth who takes up the mantle. Nick Hebbes introduces his Cholsey neighbour Steve Parkinson to the side, and the canny opening bowler steams in all season, but sadly, without luck. Parkinson is a welcome addition to the side, mainly due to his habitually violent cobbing when given out, which affords much amusement from behind the boundary rope.

Dave Shorten debuts for *The MAD* as well. An old friend of Richard Hadfield, he sadly has no information concerning Hadfield's whereabouts, rumoured to have been sighted somewhere in Africa or perhaps Walton Manor.

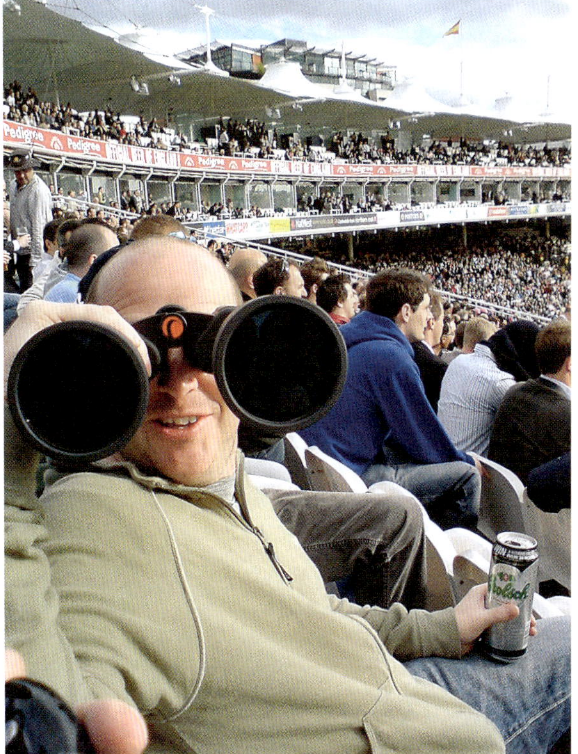

Steve is always over-joyed at being dismissed

Dan Edwards and his hat, recent victim of *The Marlborough*'s descent into *Jude*-like shiteness, score *The MAD*'s first ever century after only seven years of trying, 103 not out in the first game of the season against *Wootton & Boars Hill.* Modestly, Edwards gives credit to his wide-brimmed headwear, saying, 'It's all about you, dude.'

In a year in which once broken, the century drought becomes a flood, with two more tons from Martin Westmoreland, *The MAD* balance things out by achieving their most impressive ever batting collapse, from 99-1 to all out 108 against *Milton.*

2007

At the start of the season, tremendous news greets the team. Richard Hadfield has been found alive and well, living in Florence Park. Ranks bolstered by the return of Hadfield and the wandering Adie Fisher and Mike Clarke, and the debut of Adie Small, *The MAD* flourish.

In a season marked by flooding which sees many games cancelled and both Pembroke and Mike Reeves' house under water, Ian Howarth leads the side to an 11-6 win-loss record, their best to date.

Pembroke offering up angling opportunities

Despite their successes, it is in this year that *The MAD* discover their true place in the great cricket hierarchy, and it isn't anywhere near the top. On tour to Eastbourne, they play the *Worthing Chippendales* and face truly fast bowling for the first time. Young South African quick Straker, in the country for a trial with Sussex, takes 4-5 in a rare spell of pace bowling. Luckily *MAD* skipper Jake Hotson reverses the batting order to save the blushes of the top order.

Later in the year, *Tetsworth CC* for some reason bring their first team to Pembroke and *The MAD* get to look on as some real batsmen score some easy runs against the usual selection of *MAD* flans and jam tarts.

But it's not really about that, is it? Though it is nice to win, cricket isn't just about winning, especially at this level. It *is* about the wins and the losses, the cobs and the laughs, but it is also about those moments of rare exaltation, that feeling you get when the ball comes off the bat just right, when it sticks in the outstretched hand and stays there as you tumble to the ground, when it flies between bat and pad and knocks middle stump into the air.

Nothing gives you this feeling except cricket, getting it right, be it in front of a crowd of 28,000 at Lords, or else on a quiet poplar-ringed pitch on a Sunday afternoon in front of three people and panting dog. And that feeling means nothing without your team mates, there beside you to feel it with you. ■

2008

Antony Mann

LIKE every other year, 2008 was a year of change for *The MAD*. For without change, there is only death. While all around them the world crumbled in the wake of the Global Financial Crisis, the players of *The MAD* remained steadfast and resolute, thanks in the main to their complete lack of share portfolios and bank accounts. To make matters even worse than universal financial annihilation, probably caused by sunspot activity, in the off season the powers that be had decided that Pembroke Sports Ground would now be reserved on Sundays for Japanese students playing origami, Pembroke College old boys indulging in a little grouse spotting, freelance pig rooting, and other money-making ventures. The team was being unceremoniously turfed off their long-time spiritual home by 'The Man', and would need somewhere else to practice their weekend religion.

It proved impossible to bag another college cricket ground at such short notice, so *The MAD* ended up at the somewhat bleak and utterly mediocre Stratfield Brake Sports Ground in Kidlington. Home games in 2008 were by and large a dull affair thanks to the puddingy pitch and Kidlington-style surroundings, but there were still away games to savour visiting the usual suspects.

A glance down the list of *Mad* opponents for the year 2008 reveals teams such as *Hanney, Nomads, Wootton & Bladon, The Bodleian, Milton, RT Harris, Lemmings, Cholsey* and *OUP*. Once again, *The MAD* would face up to old foes like the redoubtable Steve 'Pooley' Poole (*Wootton & Bladon*), 'Milly' Milner, 'Macca' Mackinnon and 'Ackers' Ackland of *The Bodleian*, John 'John' Greany and The Three Bakers of *Lemmings*, and Chris 'Inspector Gadget' Heron and Andy 'Rabbits' Darley of *OU Offices*.

This was the staple diet of *The MAD*, these fixtures which came up year on year against the same old foes, the familiar faces and long-standing rivalries which gave meaning to Sunday cricket. Naturally, banter with opposing sides was always important, spiced up with the odd fist fight after a book launch or in the car park, though no deaths had as yet been reported.

John Harris considering alternative sporting pursuits

The first game of the season saw Ian Howarth don his captain's robes for the third time, as *The MAD* visited *Hanney* and figuratively spilled the home team's guts all over the sodding cow pasture. Howarth (4-16) was in the wickets as the home side was dismissed for 112, which was just as well since the skipper's *annus horribilis* with the bat was about to begin any minute now. Edwards, Carter and Hoskins knocked off the runs and *The MAD* were off to a winning start.

After a couple of cancellations due to English-style weather, *The Nomads* were next, destroyed by Mann (3-19) (including the wicket of a five-year-old) and Harris (3-40), while once again Edwards was in the runs as the side scored 144 for the win. Parkinson bowled a brilliant spell without luck. This was Andy Darley's debut match for *The MAD*, though he would keep playing for *OU Offices* long enough to gift his wicket to *Mad* bowlers on a regular basis.

With skipper Howarth selfishly off somewhere getting married to Player #88, it was left to the supposed no-hopers in the side to show how captaincy really worked. The previous Sunday Hebbes Snr had guided *The MAD* to victory over *The Nomads*, and it was he again who led the side to their third win in a row with a close win over *Wootton*

& Bladon. The run-out of *Mad* nemesis and *Wootton* talisman Steve 'Poolo' Poole for 1 did little to aid the home side's cause, and the visitors worked their way to the victory mark of 146 thanks to an 8th wicket partnership of 77 from Hoskins (41 not out) and Edwards, whose 62 not out from six thousand balls bored everyone to death but at least got the job done. No doubt Parkinson, had he played, would have bowled a brilliant spell without luck. As it was the wickets were shared around, fairly for a change.

Mad skipper Howarth at last found his way home from a Vegas chapel to grasp the poisoned chalice of captaincy, possibly drunk and definitely about to suffer a horrendous spell of poor form with the bat, to oversee a fourth win on the trot. This time it was a thorough trouncing of *The Bodleian*, who were looking in dire need of new blood. Reeves (3-13) and Hoskins (3-5) were the prime destroyers as *The Bodleian* were dismissed for a *Jude*-like 46 in 21 overs. *The MAD* knocked off the total for two wickets down, christening the forlorn wasteland that was Stratfield Brake with an emphatic win.

A loss away against *Milton* inevitably followed, a typical thrashing that saw *The MAD* chase 214-5, for a while at least, until they got to 73 and were all out. Howarth (21) and Westmoreland (17) showed they could bat a bit, and Mann (3-15) at least made an effort, but this was a dismal loss on a stinking hot day which left everyone in a crap mood. Would *The MAD* ever beat *Milton*, led to victory by an unlikely hero so drunk that he could hardly stagger to the crease? Only time would tell.

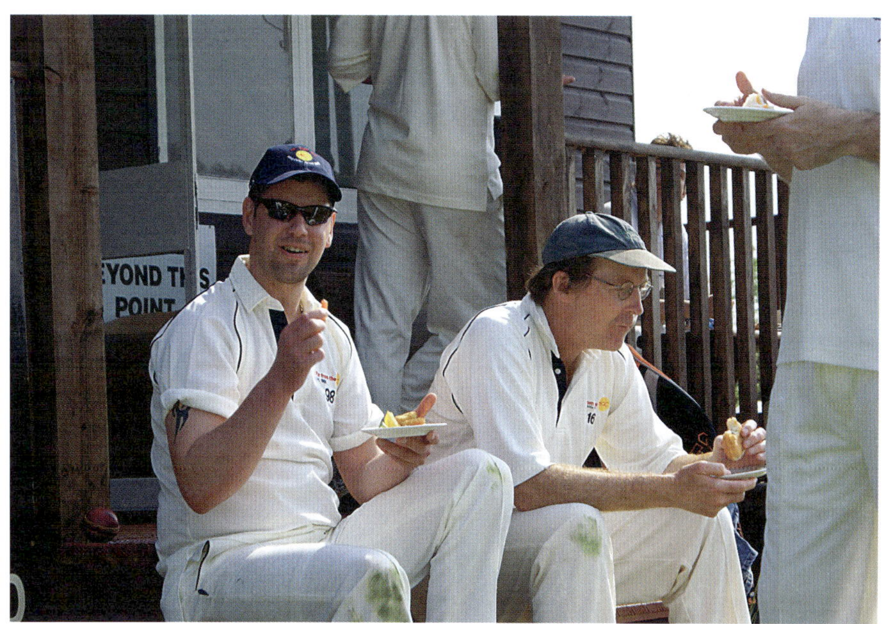

Me sitting with my favourite bunny (Andrew Darley on left)

A fine victory against *R T Harris* came next. On a slow pitch and outfield, Mann (46) played his best innings for *The MAD* since that other good one about ten years before. Together with Dobner (22) (best innings since etc etc) they steered the team to 114-9, then defended the total with aplomb, dismissing the home side for 99. Once again Mann (3-12) and Dobner (4-32) featured, and with this victory, a bogeyman of sorts had been put to rest. *R T Harris* were a strong team which *The MAD* had never before bested. Ding dong, the electrician was dead.

Another team *The MAD* had never beaten was the *Lemmings*, and it was destined to stay that way the following weekend at a windy Stratfield Brake. This was a close game though – perhaps too close for the comfort of the *Lemmings*, who on this occasion strayed perilously close to the cliff without actually leaping off. Chasing 135, *Lemmings* achieved the score with only two wickets left, thanks to useful contributions from the usual culprits, Greany and a couple of Bakers. Hebbes (3-24) was the pick of the trundlers, while a thrilling 82 with the bat from Gary Littlechild laid the foundations for what was almost, but not quite, a famous victory.

But, cometh the hour, cometh the half-pissed poet. Whatever the pros and cons of Stratfield Brake as a home ground for *The MAD* – and in all honestly the team couldn't wait to get away from it – in 2008 it was host to some famous *Mad* victories. None more so than against *Milton CC*. From a useful foundation of 0-49, the *Milton* boys fell to all out 116 thanks to two compelling spells of pie tossing from Howarth (4-28) and Hoskins (3-9 from 8 remarkable quiche-filled overs). With *The MAD* at 3-49 in reply, the visitors certainly didn't think the game was over, but local poet and pisshead Andrew Morley had other ideas. At first reluctant to leave his half-empty bottle of vodka unattended, Morlers strode to the crease and laid about the *Milton* bowling in a game-changing knock which is indelibly etched into The MAD annals of uninhibited drunken slogfests. With Dan Edwards (54 not out from eight million deliveries) playing the rock to Morley's roll, *The MAD* won the game handily by 5 wickets, a result not in the pre-game script and all the more satisfying because of it. This was the Immortal Morlers Game, and his 27 with 5 boundaries has never been bettered, by him at any rate.

Buoyed by this stirring victory, *The MAD* travelled to Blenheim Palace the following weekend on a high, rightly convinced of their infallibility, and eked out a constipated draw. Parkinson bowled, yet without luck. It was one of those games, a declaration affair, with Edwards batting seven hours for three runs to make the game safe. This was apparently the day on which Mann, who had been put at number eleven on the batting card since June 2002 and had not batted in eight years, famously called his skipper a cunt in the pub afterwards, though nobody remembers why, or even if the incident even happened.

Aiming to cash in on their good form, *The MAD* then proceeded to lose to *Cholsey* and to *R T Harris*, though not at the same time. The *Cholsey* game, away to the Cheesemen,

The greatest pissed innings of all time?

was generally woeful and barely worthy of comment, although it may possibly be worth noting that Cholsey ended the game with only six players and still won by about 200 runs. Put in to bat due to their lack of fielders, the Cheesers hit a handy 253-6, then proceeded to dismiss *The MAD* for a pathetic 61, despite the batting heroics of nobody. Stiff cheddar really.

The *R T Harris* fixture – a loss by 86 and sweet revenge for the electricians and their doughty apprentices, was marked by a record five outfield catches from Westmoreland, but little else. The curse of Stratfield Brake, not actually a curse at all, had finally struck. The tour to Mumbles followed soon after, a sodden affair enjoyed by none. A loss to *Whitland* by 5 wickets in a game played on a rain-soaked local bog preceded an abandoned game against *Mumbles* on a rain-soaked local bog which *The MAD* were about to lose when the heavens opened. Never mind, there was always mini-golf in the drizzle on a rain-soaked local bog, real golf on a bog in the rain, and the Olympics on the telly in the hotel, which had been built on a bog. Which was great if you like watching the only sports that Great Britain were any good at – rowing and cycling and swimming and not much else. The goddamn idiot who kept booking tours to Wales during the wet season was locked in a cupboard at the hotel and is there to this day, where he has accumulated a better batting average than most of the team in subsequent years.

The rain followed the side home to Oxford, and a game against *OUP* was also put out of its misery with *The MAD* on 98-2 chasing 207, thanks in the main to a century from Chris Heron. Andy Darley did not do quite so well. The last game of season 2008 saw a nondescript loss away to *Astons* while Tim Henman looked on from the mansion over the fence. Bad luck Tim, you may not have won Wimbledon, but you played the game in the right spirit, unlike all those other crumbums. Apart from the time that, in a fit of pique, you smashed a ball into a ball girl's face.

In 2008 Dan Edwards topped the batting averages with 329 at 41.13, scored at a run every ninety-three balls, with a high score of 66 not out. Gary Littlechild was next with 116 runs at 29. Martin Westmoreland scored 169 at 24.14. It was year to forget for Ian Howarth: 162 at 18. So it's a shame really that it hasn't been forgotten.

Antony Mann took 21 wickets at 11.52 with an economy rate of 2.93. He won the *Player of the Year Award* for the fourth time, and so got to keep the trophy and sell it on eBay for one quid fifty. Considering he never got a bat, something he isn't bitter about at all, it was a great achievement. Steve Dobner took 10 wickets at 14, and Ian Howarth, excelling with ball in hand to make up for his shit batting, took 13 at 19.31.

After a fighting start to the year with four wins in a row, the season had fizzled out, though a win-loss record against strong opposition of 7-6 was far from shabby. *Milton* had been beaten, *Lemmings* almost. *The Bodleian* looked to be in dire straits and destined to go the way of *The Marlborough*. In a lean season for batsmen and low team totals, the bowlers had hit their straps and got the job done more often than not, once again proving the truth of the wise words of the sadly-missed Adie Fisher. Bowlers win matches, especially bowlers who chuck pie like Adie did.

While others deputised admirably when needed, Ian Howarth was *The MAD*'s skipper, and he captained the team to yet another successful season, always with humour (often gallows) and with an evident deep love of the greatest game of all. The 'engine room' of the side, Howarth has maintained the club's ever-growing website for many years, and

Some of the dudes

would go on to expand an already bulging fixture list to three or four hundred games a season, thus rendering all previous batting and bowling records meaningless.

It was with a sad heart that Ant Mann said farewell to *The MAD* at the end of this season, consoling himself with the fact that soon he would be living in the relative paradise of Australia. Little did he know that in a scant ten years global warming and overdevelopment would have turned his idyllic mountain home west of Sydney into a desolate wasteland of 40-degree temperatures and confused, starving kangaroos.

The years he played for *The MAD* rewarded Ant Mann with some of the best days of his life, and he made many friendships that have stood the test of time.

It is no exaggeration to say that a good game of Sunday cricket, on a good ground with good team mates and good beers afterwards at a good pub, is one of the great joys of life. Coming back to Australia, The Ant/Blocker/Mangle/The Convict/The Harbourer of Dark Thoughts sought to replicate his *Jude* and *Mad* days in the local cricket comp, but though he found the odd moment of joy in the games he played, more often than not it was a bleak and ultra-competitive shit fight playing against local dickheads on artificial pitches, no cakes for tea, and no decent beers afterwards.

Though Australian league cricket might throw up a tough breed of player well-equipped to deal with adversity, hard as nails, and usually a real prick, there is not much fun to be had on those heat-seared paddocks with not a sliver of shade in sight when you are being sledged hour on hour by some teenage cockface.

There is a lot to be said for the type of cricket that *The Jude* and *The MAD* have been fortunate enough to play on the green fields of Oxford and surrounds.

Still took a bunch of wickets, though. Usually bowled. ■

vodafo
ING
KERY

2009

Ian Howarth

2009 was a transitional year for many reasons. Most notably the guy who wrote the bulk of The MAD's previous literary work, 'Not at This Level', was now gone, the call of his fellow convicts in New South Wales proving too hard to resist. Antony G. Mann had always been the sardonic, infectious and insightful heartbeat of the club since way back to its Jude days, his varied and characterful match reports an inspiration and ever-present companion. Now that scruffy and homely little three bed near Florence Park, on the aptly named Cricket Road, would lie empty. So would the detergent drawer of the washing machine where Ant would hide his house keys.

Also gone, was the chain-smoking, archetypal pub landlord and intellectual Irishman, Mr Noel Patrick Reilly, who sadly passed away the previous autumn. Without his financial support and unwavering enthusiasm, this club and *this* book might never have come to fruition. He is sorely missed by those lucky to have known him, and we should be all be very thankful for his backing of Eddie Lester's visions of a pub team some twenty years ago. Without the Noel's of this world, we'd all be bickering over the politics of getting something done without ever actually achieving anything. He became a posthumous patron.

With the slowly realised disappearances of Ade Small, John Harris and Steve Hebbes, the team's commander and chief had *also* gone. Ian Howarth hadn't left the club per se, just allowed himself to slip back into the comfortable ranks of the underperforming, a luxury afforded to the perennial whingers and doom-mongers in the team. Whether his abdication was triggered by a quite awful season with the bat, it was hard to say, but after juggling the team's insecurities and unreasonable demands for three years, he called it time. That cynically downbeat brand of northern skippering would now be replaced by that of the equally northern, slightly-less cynically downbeat Martin Westmoreland.

You can also make a case of mention for other absentees such as Huw Leggate and the unfortunate Washington family. Whilst Ian Leggate's dreadlocked brother displayed ample talent for the sport, The Washington's were on a whole new subterranean level of non-understanding bewilderment. Answering an SOS to make up numbers for an end of season trip to Aston Tirrold, a game of cricket plugged the gaping hole of a family breakup, or maybe it didn't. Now whilst Andy copped a second ball duck, he at least knew he had to lift his bat to strike the ball. His son Alex didn't, somehow scoring a single off a stationary blade as his helmet flopped over his face.

With the UK economy finally coming out of recession, the cricketing landscape would change yet further with the befriending of a groundsman called Dan and relocation of The MAD back to central Oxford (whence it came). Brasenose College Sports Ground was a world away from the soulless vacuum which had been Stratfield Brake in Kidlington. The student's indifference to making full use of their pretty little ground in summer working triumphantly in the club's favour. Whereas previously one would be sat with a hangover amongst a blustery panoramic nothingness, now you could nurse a hangover in a striped deckchair, your mood uplifted by church bells and the sound of jazz music floating across the pitch as Salter's steamers sailed on by. We'd found a proper home, one which wasn't our home, but nonetheless *felt* like home. One steeped in history with David Cameron looking down on your teas from his eighties team photo hung high on the pavilion wall.

The MAD's new home of Brasenose. Cricket with soul.

Pre-season nets have always been an important part of The MAD calendar. An opportunity to renew friendships that had died or shrivelled during winter, with the rediscovery of all the aches and pains you bitch about over summer. Bowlers are summarily flogged, batsmen look way better than they actually are (you can't be caught in nets), whilst some of the guys just slope around the edges preferring a chinwag and a fag outside. Then after the sudden jolt to your metabolism, it's time to reset your circuitry and rehydrate in the pub thereafter, ruminating over each other's potential Fantasy cost. At this time of the year it's *all* about fantasy, a world we don't live in but wish we did half the time. Who out of this dysfunctional mix of has-beens and never-will-be's is going to have *that* defining season? Who is going to justify your imaginary cash and confidence in them? And who is to be avoided at all cost as their season collapses amidst the cricketing ignominy of ducks, run outs, drops, spankings and gaffs a plenty?

Whilst an increase in off-season paunch can be blamed squarely on the pub, these much maligned social hubs have many benefits. You can obviously get pissed, you can bicker and have a good satisfying moan *and* you can also occasionally make new friends. These friends are often the lifeblood of Sunday cricket, the bodies that fill the holes when others decide to leave, retire or simply give up because they're so effing crap. These friends are also the prime source of new contacts, fixtures and eventually new rivalries. *Never* underestimate the importance of the pub.

David Emerson never underestimated the importance of the pub, which is why hc became The MAD's marquee signing at the season's beginning. Following nets, the affable and thoughtful Kiwi was poached after being chatted up by the bar, naturally being promised a good bat up the order. He came highly touted by his wannabee agent and university devotee, Andrew Darley, who professed Dave to have an excellent eye when slaughtered and also halfway decent with the ball. Whether this eye was for the ladies, it was hard to assess, though his obvious good looks had him quickly labelled as the club's Tesco Value Brad Pitt. He debuted at the picturesque ground of Wootton & Boars Hill, where on a warm and breezy April afternoon, Mr Westmoreland's inaugural match in charge ended in failure after slumping to 16-4 chasing 160 plus. Dave impressed with his medium pace, before joining an illustrious ensemble of MAD men before him by bagging a *duck on debut.* Respect where it's due, he didn't fanny about during that one ball at the crease, batting at number eleven.

Things improved for our new skipper the following week, his pugnacious unbeaten fifty guiding the team to a rousing 10 wicket win against Cholsey CC. His partnership with the infrangible Dan Edwards was all the more impressive, given the pitch surpassed even the worst expectations, riddled as it was with craters from a coalition airstrike, and marked with the pits and gouges of the previous day's Cholsey Annual Stomping Competition.

Conditions couldn't have been better for The MAD's first game at Brasenose however, where a low scoring game is only remembered for Edwards' outrageous show of pique

A golden debut awaited Mr Emerson at Wootton & Boars Hill.

and helmet throwing after a debatable LBW decision. We can talk at great length about LBWs and indeed we do (at great length), but in the spirit of the game, we should just accept the umpire's decision, sigh inwardly and depart in a dignified manner for the sanctuary of the changing rooms†. Once there, out of sight, you can call everyone a cheating bastard before launching into a diatribe about the stupid prick who just gave you out. Even if you thought you were out, which of course nobody else needs to know.

Inclement weather and a round of impromptu golf would occupy the following weeks, with cricket finally returning against the *new* yet Old East Oxford. Following Edwards' surly behaviour (LBW) last time out, this time it was Howarth muddying the team's name, the poor umpire forced to defend a routine plumb in front. Fortunately Ian's distemper didn't take the gloss off what was a magnificent unbeaten 101* from the aforementioned Edwards, who in scoring what was then the sixth MAD century, also faced more balls (130) than anyone had or has since. Dan was the ultimate counter of balls in an over, a man who would just *know* intuitively when to scamper that single off the final ball. A partnership was all about him. The indomitable anchor and hog of an innings, he simply gorged on dot balls like a psychotic Pacman. However, the MOTM award would eventually be shared on that day, following Dave Emerson's excellent 5-25, a glowing testament to his bowling under the influence at six stumps.

---

† *Around this time The MAD attempted to make the cricketing experience more pleasant for spectators and everyone else. This was achieved by creating an environment to which parents could safely bring their children without fear that they would be subject to the petulant outbursts of aggrieved players. Central to this was the 'club ethos' introduced by James Hoskins, which demanded respect for ones fellow players, opposition, spectators and in particular umpires. Players would be heavily fined for displays of dissent, antagonism or argument. As part of this agreement, the changing rooms were deemed a safe haven, out of bounds to anyone but the players, so they could go and act like toddlers without fear of recrimination.*

Sunday, June 14 was no ordinary day. Indeed it is a date lithographed into MAD folklore. A brilliant and satirical match report from Nick Hebbes likened the game to the slaughter seen on the front lines in WWI. It was either famous or infamous depending on your disposition, but indelible nonetheless. Following Westmoreland's fateful decision to field first after being given the option (why, oh why, Martin?), the team were treated to 33.2 overs of the most brutal, pyrotechnical hitting ever seen, especially at *this* level. Under a maelstrom of bruised and battered cricket balls, cars reversed and disappeared from view as watching spectators fled to a nearby (or not so nearby pub). Nothing and nobody was spared, including a kid's playground and the optic bottles in the Tetsworth CC pavilion. It was all James Hoskins' fault, having the sheer audacity to bowl the openers and unleash hell. The hitting was so barbaric that at one point, a Howarth over that had just gone for 34 was itself in danger of being eclipsed by one from Nick Hebbes (four sixes off his first four balls). There would be no let up as Steve Dobner watched one pinball around a parking space after leaving a hole in Andrew Darley's right hand. In total, West Indian T20 supremo Hyron Shallow, smacked 18 sixes and 15 fours in his 182 retired out of a total of 358-8. In fairness, the home side did throw some shit down in allowing The MAD to reach a hundred in reply, before a second onslaught from Hyron's stablemate, Mr O. Jackson (7-22) ended the game. This dicking to end all uber-tonkings ended in a barrage of wrong 'uns, doosras, darts and balls that hadn't even got a name. Fittingly, the final gunfire saw Emerson record a diamond duck as he was ran out at the non-strikers end by none other than Mr Shallow. A wreath of 207 poppies signalling the margin of defeat is laid at the ground in each passing year.

358 runs later…

The Tetsworth Batting Massacre saw to it that Martin needed time off to convalescence, and perhaps Vice Skipper Dobner wished he had too, overseeing as he did a shambolic six wicket reverse at home to the Lemmings and yet *another* unsuccessful trip to Bloxham to play Milton CC. The latter defeat was despite Mike Reeves' left arm excellence in returning 5-29 and Howarth carrying his bat for a dogged 74 not out.

After Thornton Smith's late slog, The MAD may well have chased the total down that day, but the hypochondriac which is Steve Dobner did his hamstring and Jake Hotson copped one to the jaw. Asking *how* bad the damage was to his face, Emerson examined the wound before replying to the bandaged Hotson that "he could probably put his cock (in the hole)."

It wasn't all doom and gloom of course, spirits were lifted by a routine T20 beat down of the Bodleian, and of course there was the fun and originality of a tri-team tournament at Cutteslowe Park involving Wootton & Boars Hill (W&BH) and the Oxford University Offices (OUO). With glorious weather and a grandiose barbeque in evidence, a fitting finale saw W&BH tying the F15 final chasing The MAD's 88 all out. The FFTMCC could and probably should have won the tournament off the last ball of the day, but Umpire Emerson correctly ruled that keeper Geoff Carter didn't have the ball to hand when removing the bails (silly old sod). There were many stars of this day, including the erratic and fictional Mike Clarke (20*), Aussie man-child JP Collins (his 27 including 3 sixes) and the legendary guru of always being right, Ade Fisher (13* and 11 in the two innings respectively) and of course you could never look past the delicious leg spinning tarts of Ian Leggate (3-0-20-2 in the final).

Sunday teams have always been the most susceptible to capitulation and disappearing into a blackened void, never to be remembered. They rarely have their own ground, are largely unsupervised and a youth policy is considered signing up a middle-aged pisshead at the end of the bar. The teams grow old as one, largely ignorant to their dodgy knees and a drop in their stock. It's all about camaraderie, enthusiasm and a bloody good drink with your mates (and of course time away from your family). So when that guy who seemingly does everything suddenly decides he's had enough, you're all in the shit. This was the case with the weekend University Offices outfit, a team slowly haemorrhaging at the seams under the tough regime of Skipper Nickel, and there was nothing club dogsbody and multi-team gun for hire Andrew Darley could do to arrest the decline. Fractious infighting and an absence of anyone giving a f___, meant that wonderful memories of tours to Newcastle, Belfast and Cardiff were superseded by an embarrassing swansong in Oxfordshire. This bastard half-breed of a tour sounded the OUO death-knell and a MAD lifeboat was dispatched to haul the ringers from the sea. Most drowned, but they were the ones who couldn't bat, bowl or stand at the front of the queue at the bar.

After joining the club back in 2008, the delightfully offbeat and leftfield Ian Leggate shone through as a religious devotee to the sport without ever surmounting the gap between enthusiastic and plainly useful. This was set to change on one of the greatest stages of all, the baroque surroundings belonging to the Duke & Duchess of Marlborough, Blenheim Palace. In front of an audience of curious Pan-American tourists and affluent members of a Porsche convention, Gonzo's breakthrough figures of 5-45 could have been even better had his team mates not opted to dip their hands in butter beforehand. A magnificent finish to a timed encounter saw Westmoreland's (73)

Ian Leggate (back row, 2nd from left) accompanied by his dedicated companion, a bottle of booze

heroics ultimately undone as James Hoskins failed to hit the final ball for four. Actually, he failed to hit the *second* final ball for four also, as the previous one was declared a no ball.

Timed cricket seems to divide opinion like no other, apart from all the other formats of this bewildering sport (which also divide opinion). In short, the team who bat first gets to bat as long as they want unless they are all out, which often isn't the case as there is no real impetus to take risks and get the f___ on with it. A calculated declaration is thus enforced to leave the opposition a finite time with which to chase down the total. How this is calculated is usually formulated in the skipper's head, and to understand that equation would be to peel back the layers of an onion and probably unearth a world of wrong. If he hates the jumped up arseholes that represent the surly opposition, he could very well have his team bat all day. Some have. Blenheim Park CC gauged things perfectly.

As President Obama began withdrawing troops from Iraq, rain would force a similar abandonment of an Astons CC game before The MAD enjoyed a purple patch prior to touring. Fine Sunday victories were complemented with the T20 scalps of Appleton and

St Clements. With Howarth resurgent unencumbered by captaincy, Dave Shorten was materialising into the complete all-rounder we always knew he could be. A bruising slog of 41 would be complemented by the inswinging figures of 7-3-8-3, a spell which sliced clean through a much vaunted Wootton & Bladon top order. About this time, Dave was also finishing his dream of building his own house on Oxford's Mulholland Drive (Boars Hill), whilst becoming an instantly recognisable TV star with a family-based reality show. Was there anything our eccentric, earthy bespectacled hero could not do? Well, yes, but we'll come back to that at the end of this chapter….

The tour to the market town of Louth was engineered by Steve Parkinson, who taking up a self-imagined ambassadorial role, promised to open doors for the team in and around his old stomping ground. These doors mostly belonged to failing nightclubs and blood stained pubs, but one impressive door belonged to Louth CC's elegant new pavilion. In celebration of its opening earlier that year, the league club organised a weekend festival of cricket which consisted of a Thursday "amuse bouche" pasting of the Far from the MCC, prior to the main course where their muscular 1st XI bullied the diminutive England ladies cricket team.

Aside from being drunk most of the time, gambling at poker until the early hours and singing about Louth Ladies in the shadows of the tallest church spire in England, other memories include the argument† around Captain Reeves' batting order on the Saturday, Martin Westmoreland hooking a ball into his face and Ian Leggate salsa dancing with the England cricket captain Claire Taylor (this after he'd finally extricated himself from the back of Mr Shorten's padlocked works van). It was a memorable Tour as *all* tours are, and the team left Lincolnshire on a high after Thornton Smith captained the team to an eight wicket win over Legbourne CC on the way home. This victory that would prove a precursor to a six year drought of touring success and also a stage for Nick Hebbes to do something with the Legbourne wicket and a fennel, for reasons which are known only to him and his brother, Steve. If it was some sort of offering to the cricketing gods, they were listening, as he was able to boast that "the next one is going through the club house door" before delivering on that promise to scoop the Champagne Moment of the Season. The gods then pissed on his chips seeing him out on 48.

On return to The Shires it is de rigueur to experience a predictably gloomy and

† *The argument, if one can call it that, centred on a widespread malaise within the team for opening or batting up the order. Despite Mike's vested endeavours and talking positively about chasing 240 over the tea interval, he ended up losing his temper and storming off shouting "I give up!" The team ended up picking itself with no fewer than eight players vying for the coveted number six position. Number six is the celebrated spot in a Tour batting line-up that both insulates a batsman from any decent opening bowlers whilst allowing ample time to shake off a hangover. Moreover, there is usually adequate time to compile a decent score whilst feasting off the rubbish (lesser bowlers and pie). There were no surprises to see Steve Parkinson settling into the hallowed position, chest puffed out and coasting to 26 not out.*

Claire Taylor only too happy to have some idiot photo bomb her with a copy of The MAD's previous book

systematic downturn in form and this year was no different. An inept humbling in Cholsey prefaced a trip to the dystopian wastelands of Holton, where those present that day still wish they *never* were. Given that the playing fields had long since been given up to footballing chavs and feral dogs, The MAD lost out to a vapid R. T. Harris team fasting for Ramadan. In bouts of withering rain on an artificial strip more suited to

Fortunately Martin was never The MAD's poster boy before this incident

Grange Hill, a reduced over contest was plagued by stumps stood in sand, an inability to decipher a boundary and a complete absence of teas. Hell was probably a less depressing alternative to that day, with James Hoskins' resembling a bloodied butcher from drying the ball. We never went back.

In all, 24 players represented the team during Martin's first season in charge, a promising one that saw 10 wins against 11 losses and only tailed off towards the end. James Hoskins proved the most turn-outable of those that turned out, his 24 appearances good enough to see him sweep nearly every award at the end of season popularity contest (which drunkenly doubles as The MAD AGM). James' haul of 33 wickets at a paltry average of just 17.00 would prove infinitely more popular than the umpire-hating efforts with the bat of Messrs Edwards (641 runs at 45.79) and Howarth (572 runs at 47.67). Being complicit with the laws of cricket and not behaving like a cock really does pay dividends you see? Westmoreland also led by example with a Clubman-esque 366 runs at 22.88, backed up by his dutiful enforcer Mr Dobner, whose all-round resurgence netted 256 runs at 18.29 and 21 wickets at 22.71. Steve also avoided any altercations of note and threatened nobody's welfare in any adjacent car parks.

The superlative FFTMCC 5-a-side football team

With Chairman Bullock's gavel sounding the end of the evening, nay the season, it should have all been packed away in kitbags and left to stink in the loft, but not quite. You see there was just enough time for Michael Jackson to overuse his meds and Mr Shorten to enrol the club in a fanciful 5-a-side football league. Reasoning on continued friendship during the darkened weeks to come, Dave inexplicably booked The MAD's stuttering enthusiasts in a tourney for diehard 20-somethings. The lamentable outcome over the course of a nine week mauling was overseen by 70s Manager, Mr T. P. W. Smith. Decked out in a sheepskin coat with a four pack of Stella to hand, Thorn would bark out his orders like Jack Regan of The Sweeney, masterminding a final goal difference of minus 98. The low point of this whole debacle played out in sub-zero temperatures at Tilsley Park, came in the final game in which The MAD had offered to forfeit, thus handing their opponents a 10-0 win under the rules of the tournament. The opposition declined this offer on the grounds they needed a goal difference of +12 to secure second place. The MAD inevitably complied by shipping a further 13 goals. In future the team would be sticking solely to cricket. ■

Spam
99

2010

Mike Reeves

2010 may not have been a seminal year for the FFTMCC but certainly marked a significant development point with many of the debutants that year (not counting Ross Maher, but more on him later) going on to become stalwarts of the club. David Emerson had joined the team in 2009 and by 2010 was something of a fixture. He was therefore asked to mine his contacts list for anyone else of a cricketing persuasion. He searched his office at Centrica / British Gas and came up with James Pearson and Gary Timms. Also significant this year was members of OU Offices looking to broaden their horizons and thus Patrick Mellor and Chris Roberts were also welcomed on board.

First game of the season was against Horspath CC. If recollection serves correctly (it doesn't), Ian Howarth (Spam) pushed hard to sell this fixture to a sceptical committee, on the grounds that it was at a lovely location and definitely *not* the shithole of the Horspath recreation ground next door. Horspath were and remain a flourishing league team, boasting a number of sides at various levels. Despite the talk of an overseas professional there were assurances that they understood that we were a bunch of Sunday slobs and would put out a team accordingly. I think we knew the game was up as we arrived and saw the advertising hoardings and maybe Aussie Alister Gibbins didn't get the memo as he smashed 78 including eight sixes and then took 4-12. The game was also notable for the non-appearance of the Harlow globetrotter, Steve Dobner, who was stuck in Tenerife due to the Icelandic ash cloud†. If this were a Hollywood story of a young man rejected by society who gets his one shot at greatness, we could say that Steve's absence handed a debut to James Pearson (a man whose

---

† *Whilst missing the season's opener was just about forgivable, having his brother-in-law stand in as childminder for a self-promoted trip to Wembley was not. Having forcibly sold numerous dodgy tickets to watch his beloved Saracens smash Harlequins in the Rugby Cup Final, Gary vowed never to play for The Club again after failing to control the "adults" who slopped beer over fellow spectators, swore in unison around minors and found it titillating to run amok in the stadium fountains outside. These "adults" also kept Gary waiting for hours before kick-off to accommodate an undulating piss-up on the way to London.*

No caption required....

rumoured military background was at odds with his apparent inability to get up in the morning), who grabbed the opportunity with both hands producing excellent figures of 7-1-31-3 and giving Howarth out LBW. In reality I guess he was due to play in any case.

The MAD bounced back in game two with an emphatic win against Wootton & Boars Hill including an unbeaten century partnership between Howarth and Hebbes. On to game three then as the NoMADs of Swindon were welcomed to Cutteslowe Park. The game was a jolly affair which will be remembered for the one and only appearance of a certain Ross Maher.

Like most Sunday teams, The MAD has always been built from a core team of enthusiastic organisers around which a series of more peripheral individuals orbit. There are however none more peripheral than Ross. Where he came from I'm not quite sure, but I think he was a frequent if not ever present at nets. I don't remember him as a stand out player, but once he'd shelled out for some kit, the assumption was that he'd slot into the team and become a regular throughout the 2010 season. We've all had games to forget, but generally that doesn't diminish our enthusiasm or determination to turn out the following weekend, not so Ross. He dropped a sitter, bagged a golden and that was it, the last we heard from him. I hope you're not trapped down a well Ross, or wandering around a foreign land with amnesia, although considering that I think it was you who asked to be removed from the infamous MAD email list some months later, I think you're alright.

Ah yes, the infamous MAD mailing list. It's like the Hotel California, you can check out, but you can never leave. When wanting to email the whole team, to deploy some witticism, hit 'reply all' rather than 'reply' or do whatever it is that Andrew Darley does with email, one generally just looks for a recent or not so recent email from anyone in the team. Hence there is a multitude of lists of various age and accuracy. Getting yourself removed from all of these is a challenge for the modern age.

Game four, away at Wootton & Bladon saw the shortest non-game in MAD history. This is again a scenario familiar to any Sunday cricketer. The weather forecast has been for showers and periods of heavier rain. You wake up on Sunday morning to leaden skies, but still there's an optimism which drives you to think that there might be some play. Maybe a shortened 20-20 or a 10-10 or a 5-5. Maybe the forecasters are wrong and it'll clear up. So the decision is made to prepare the teas, pack the kit bag and head out to a far flung corner of Oxfordshire and wait. And wait some more. For the record, the game lasted all of eight balls, during which Dan Edwards scored an impressive 12* and Nick at least got a not out. Inevitably and not for the first or last time, the teams repaired to a local pub before driving home in bright sunshine. The MAD didn't learn its lesson about games of this type until another disastrous trip to Wootton three years later.

The game was also notable for the most uninspiring MAD debut since Ross in the previous game. Welcome and TFC (thanks for coming) to Chris 'Tall Bob' Roberts. Some nicknames stick and some don't. Bob's stuck like a limpet to duct tape. I think it was Spam (another sticker) who took one look at Chris (as nobody now calls him) and immediately and inexplicably thought of Fat Bob from the Fast Show. Bob's nickname

Martin loving his trip to Woodstock...."

has stuck to such an extent that even players who have played with him for the seven intervening years still struggle for his real name when requested by an opposition scorer. Bob made his proper debut in the following game against OUP, scoring only six and picking up the buffet award. Still he went on to become a much loved friend and fellow player enjoying the camaraderie of Sunday and midweek games, developing a close bond with like-minded individuals and eventually giving his life some meaning and purpose. So in your face Ross. The game was remarkable for an OUP collapse, going from 89-2 to 139 all out and losing by nine runs.

At the tail end of May the country got used to the idea of a coalition government and The MAD suffered a customary debacle against Milton CC, a game mentionable only because Mr Darley demonstrated he could swing the willow for an amazing 52 off 51 balls out of a total of 124 off 233 balls.

In to June and against a backdrop of the World Cup and England shipping four goals against Germany, the first T20 of the year saw The MAD cruise to victory against OUP at Jesus College, in part thanks to James Pearson (31*) showing he could also bat. June was a topsy-turvy month form wise with big wins against Old East Oxford and the Bodleian but losses to Lemmings and a Marsh XI and an absolute thumping against Appleton CC. The Old East Oxford game is somewhat legendary due to a classic match report from Steve Parkinson highlighting the almost simultaneous failures of the England football team and Ian Howarth. In the report, Steve brought the reader's attention to several words, such as schadenfreude, that have no direct translation in English. However, even Steve, with his obvious mastery of language, failed to come up with a word in any dialect to describe the act of getting out in a ridiculous and self-negligent manner, such as Spam did on 99, for the second time in his career. That it was a match winning performance, bettered only on five occasions in the history of the club at that point, was not lost on his teammates as they fell about laughing on the boundary. Also, the fact that he was wearing his shirt number of 99, assigned to him after the previous aberration in 2005 is, as the French say "ironique".

During a delightful evening at Mansfield Road against the Bodleian, The MAD gave a debut to 11 year old Jack Cox, a young chap under the tutelage of Thornton Smith who barely stood taller than his kneecaps. Like all impressionable young men, Jack quickly learned how to score a duck, drop a ball and use adjectives for his team mates you can only find in the Chamber's dictionary. He was cruelly denied a pint at the games conclusion and like the aforementioned Ross Maher, was never seen again.

When it wasn't about Derrick Bird and Raoul Moat, the start of July was all about The MAD's left hander and big head Mike Reeves. First he single-handedly beat a Marsh XI with figures of 4-0-14-4 before smashing 20 off 8 balls to bring the team home with an over to spare. He then struck 85 against the Astons to the bemusement of Ralph Smith in a century partnership with Martin Westmoreland. His teammates were so delighted with his prowess and modesty that a protest vote was quickly organised against a Man

Thorn receives batting lessons off little Jack

of the Match award. There then followed his amazing dismissal against the OU offices. Amazing, because it was a scarcely believable, leaping one-handed catch from one Patrick Anthony Seymour Mellor. It is worth noting that the opposition that day also included skipper Andrew Darley, Mark Rundle, Chris (Bob) Roberts and the very first encounter with a certain Gary Timms.

The end of July saw a remarkable game at Brasenose College against Cholsey. It started with Jake Hotson succumbing to a frequent dancing injury, opening the door for Thornton Smith to make what was described as a long overdue fifty as The MAD reached 193 all out in 38.3 overs. In reply, the visitors were cruising at 156-2 until Dave Emerson ripped through them to record the first genuine (i.e. not spread over two matches) MAD hat-trick. He then continued, along with Dan Edwards to reduce Cholsey to 163 for 8. Having snatched victory from the jaws of defeat, The MAD then

T. P. W. Smith playing perfectly through the V.

put a little garnish on the victory, provided a full bodied Merlot to accompany it and served it up as a tasty snack. Cholsey won with one wicket and three balls to spare.

August and the team welcomed another new comer to its ranks. Gary Timms played his first game for The MAD in a (then) record run-chase against Wootton & Bladon, notching the winning run after an all-too-familiar MAD collapse. Gary would like it preserved for all time that his first game was number 211 and his squad number is 112. Palindrome-tastic. Later in August, against Blenheim, Aussie gun-for-hire Jenner Collins battered 102 before being bowled by a nine year old, whilst Nick Hebbes was run out for 1 after 17 balls. In Judas† news, James Pearson took four wickets.

August also saw a tour to Lyme Regis. One match was lost to the weather, but still there were enough notable incidents to make it a classic. There was of course 'that' bed incident. There's the nearest we've ever come to getting in a fight with some locals, before Nick Hebbes talked some sense in to everybody. Ian Leggate was in magnificent form as fines chairman, fining Howarth for 'being a c___' and then fining him for the same offence a few minutes later. Ian Howarth, not just a c___, but a 'c___ times two', is something that will live with me. The Saturday was taken up by getting pissed in stages and watching a rather dull league game at Sidmouth CC, where despite the ground being all of twenty yards from our guest house, Tour organiser James Hoskins had inexplicably failed to secure a game at. The day would be partially enlivened by an impromptu MAD Top Trumps competition and Dan Edwards repeatedly telling one of their openers to get on with it against some rather fearsome looking bowling.

Matt Bullock was for the first and most certainly last time, sharing a bedroom on tour with young Ben Mander. Benjamin was being at his most 'entertaining' best and keeping Matt awake until the early hours, not that Matt harboured any ill feeling. Well, not until he triggered him LBW the next day to one that was passing high and wide over leg stump and hitting Mander on his left nipple.

Star of the tour was undoubtedly the aforementioned James Hoskins, who collected his one and only fifty on the first day against Honiton CC. You can't fault James for backing himself and after promising a fifty with the Mongoose, he delivered and thus doubled the fines for *all* his team mates. James was instrumental in The MAD Olympics too, featuring a range of physical and mental challenges over the course of the weekend. I believe it was all decided in the final event 'Frisbeer' a combination of Frisbee and, erm… beer of course. Steve Dobner had a stellar tour, first getting caught on the boundary when anything else would have probably won us the game, and then registering his displeasure (permanently) in the Honiton changing room. The second game saw Mr Reeves launching a huge six through the trees and on to the badge at the front of his Volvo. Oh, how we laughed (but not anywhere near Steve you understand). Dave Emerson simply had a Stella tour.

† *Records and references recorded under the title, Judas, are those attributed to a club member of The MAD who has guested for the opposition.*

Before the sands of the season ran out, a remarkable match in Aston Tirrold would end in a dramatic tie. This match wouldn't be remembered for the longest partnership in MAD history (Edwards and Howarth somehow navigating 192 balls on a pudding adding 94), nor for Thornton Smith filling in for the opposition (unbeaten) or the last Astons batsman M. Moore being bowled by a pie with the scores level. No, this game would be remembered by the enforced ending of The MAD innings at the tea interval, by an unknown local bylaw stating "if the home team are bored of fielding, just pull the plug." Now that would usually be fine after 51 overs (another record), however like the majority of us, our chairman of two decades lives and plays for the day where things simply go right. Having switched through the gears, there Matt Bullock sat staring blankly at his cream scones and cup of tea, sawn off in his prime just nine runs short of a maiden fifty. One day, Matthew. One day.

During 2010 we also said goodbye (but only in the metaphorical sense, in reality, like most cricketers leaving teams, he simply stopped responding to emails) to Andrew Morley. As we know, Sunday cricket is a broad church, appealing to a range of abilities, everything from the ringers who should and sometimes do also play league cricket, through the wannabees, who played well at school and then gave it up for a few years. Then to the athletes, who play a range of sports and try to bring their best squash forehand or golf swing to the cricket pitch. Then to those who simply have nothing better to do on a Sunday. Finally we come to Andrew Morley, perhaps the worst player ever to turn out for the FFTMCC (other than Ross Maher obviously). In fact the person least suited to any sport I've ever seen. Think your sister trying to play pool.

A man and his Goose

Matt Bullock's half century that never was

Think when your family once went to the beach and Aunty Joyce joined in a game of football.

My main experience of cricket with Andrew was playing against him for the Marlborough House. I remember one Sunday at Pembroke I was batting and he was as usual standing at square leg, when I spooned the ball straight to him. Often when you send the ball in the air in the direction of a fieldsman, time seems to slow down and you go through a range of emotions. First there's the sickening feeling that you've cocked it up. Then there's the hope that the fielder will drop it. This is heightened if the fielder has to turn and run away from the wicket, or at least start pedalling backwards. In this scenario I always think there is a better than 50/50 chance of survival. Then comes the disappointment or elation as the catch is either taken or dropped. On this occasion, I don't remember any of these emotions. It was so straight to him that there was no possibility that it wouldn't be taken and yet I don't think he even got a hand to it. As it says on the website, Andrew is largely the reason why the club had to start getting insurance as there were genuine fears for his safety every time he went out to play. Andrew played his last game for The MAD on 16th June, scoring 3 not out against the Marsh XI. My time with the FFTMCC didn't overlap that of Andrew very much, but I understand what he lacked in cricketing ability he more than made up for in drinking and poetry. Andrew you are missed and are welcome to come and watch from the boundary any time.

At the other end of the cricketing ability spectrum was of course Gary Littlechild. Again, I'd first met Gary whilst playing against him in my pre-FFTMCC days. Gary was a vociferous wicket keeper who brought an intensity to Sunday cricket that was something of a surprise to opposition and team mates alike. His legendary shout of 'the line is mine' displayed eyesight and an understanding of the laws which went beyond most of the umpires required to cast judgement under his protests. He was a formidable batsman and a career average of 40.00 from 30 matches puts him almost in the ringer category. Along with his brother in law, Steve Dobner, he formed the Essex barrow boys and eventually the round trip proved too much. He made his last outing for The MAD against Appleton on 22nd August. It's doubtful that we've seen the last of Gary or his orange gloves, however taking the Wembley fiasco into account, maybe we have.

The last of the trio of retirees in 2010 was Tony 'Doc' Mander, who played his last game against Blenheim Park on 8th August. Tony and his son Ben had been regulars with the club almost from the start in 1999. Tony continues to support the club financially and turns up periodically to see the team play, particularly when he has nothing better to do, which is a rare occurrence, for him anyway.

One man bestrode 2010 like a cricketing behemoth. Martin Westmoreland played 26 games, the most of any player. He captained the team, scored 423 runs at 24.88, his most in any season, took 29 wickets, his most in any season and also took 11 catches and a run out, which again was the best for the season. He was the shoe-eist of shoe-ins for the Player of the Season award.

So what do we remember from 2010? Kim's wonderfully decorated cakes? Thirteen wins, a record which stood until the modern era of 2015. Spam scoring 552 runs at 29.05, beating Dan (551 at 26.24) to highest scorer by one. Mike Reeves 332 runs at 25.54. Dave Emerson's breakthrough haul of 28 wickets at 19.57. Mainly some notable debuts and a stable and successful team. Good times. ■

Tony is unsure what a glove is doing on his hand

2011

Ian Howarth

2011 offered a glimpse into the future as a dusty drape was lowered ever so gently onto Ed Lester's naive but beautiful Jude the Obscure. No longer could this Oxford pub team be solely underscored by the blasé weekend slob thing, the club had moved with the times and in doing so had embraced the vulgar impetuosity of T20 cricket. Fracturing down the middle and now serving two separate captains, Mr Westmoreland's merry band of diehard pissheads still earned the weekend bread and butter, but the gaudy midweek baton was now with Skipper Hotson, The MAD's first T20 Head Honcho elect. Tearing up the time-honoured script of an organised batting line-up and a diligently constructed total, Jake's leadership would usher in pool systems, advanced calculus and unscripted do-or-die decisions based on an insomniac's two hours sleep maximum. Was it chaos or chaos theory? Bowlers were batsman, batsmen were bowlers and if you stopped to think, you really hadn't a clue what the hell was going on.

With a surfeit of cricket in the year that Osama Bin Laden finally met his seventy two virgins, new recruits to bolster an ageing squad were a priority. Nick Hebbes had relocated somewhere unknown and the Mander Clan were unavailable for comment. Long before Lee Grant Ainsworth ever decided he'd had enough of the soulless drudgery of league cricket, he guested for The MAD in their season opener against Horspath CC. He displayed a skillset that would enrich the club in years to come, moaning throughout and stroking a majestic fifty on debut, a feat only equalled by two other MAD debutants and since one of them is fictional (Richard Hadfield) and the other a ringer (John Greany of the Lemmings), Lee was probably the first. If one were to be cruel, then the only black mark against the cantankerous and infectious Ainsworth is the fact he is left handed and therefore considered handicapped. Much akin to that other anomaly Mike Reeves, although it must be said (by Mike Reeves) that Lee is not a true leftie, given that he bowls the "normal" way. His ability to use a potato peeler and to play polo is unknown.

Another future stalwart making his first MAD splash was the seasoned and affluently named medium-paced tearaway, Jon Newman-Robson. Another refugee from the

The MAD are unwilling to lose their prize asset (Lee)

weekend OU Offices, 'Salad' somehow transferred a nickname that nobody really understands to this day. Going wicketless with a (Greek?) side-order of tonk, our oblique blonde toiled as Oxfordshire's finest battered up 300-5 declared, before becoming one of five ducks as the FFTMCC crashed from 53-0 to 100 all out. Jon's five ball virtuoso effort with the bat would however ensure his lifelong membership to the much vaunted *Duck on Debut* club. It was a debut to relish and a testament to Lee and Jon's graveyard humour that they remain a constant to this day.

The following week, Rob Eaglestone became The MAD's thirty second Duck on Debut as the team recorded their first win of the season at the lofty Wootton & Boars Hill. James Pearson (71*) would announce his future potential with the bat during a revelatory mix of defence and aggression, helped in no small part by Mr Newman, who this time got off the mark.

There then followed a small gap in The MAD fixture list, an intentional one which allowed for that brilliant advert or trailer your remember long after the main event. The FFTMCC had been invited to a May Day 6-a-side cricket festival in Appleton. The club are often invited to such events and we mistakenly think it's because we're such bloody nice chaps. We are (I think), but we're also bloody good losers and we tend to drink more than any other club as well. It's a win win for the hosts, making money on the beer and burgers† and also progressing in the tourney at the expense of that shit pub team. Cumnor Youth, Wootton Paunch and an Appleton Pissed VI did exactly that, progress at expense of that crappy little pub team, but not before a MAD VI became the only team on the day where all six batsmen were dismissed (in less than three overs). Last batsman Ian Leggate managed preposterously to run himself out whilst batting on his own. He later claimed not to have heard a call by his non-existent partner.

On resumption of more recognisable cricketing activities, Dave Emerson hogged the headlines in Swindon's Nomad country with a buffet strewn 5-for. This notable achievement foreshadowed one of those exhilarating performances which leave The MAD scratching their heads for reasons to continue playing. Debutant Mark (Psycho) Rundle became the thirty third esteemed Duck on Debut as the team were literally bowled out on a lumpy school pitch in Woodstock. All ten batsmen heard the death rattle against Wootton & Bladon and all ten used the excuse of getting plastered at Mike Reeves' wedding reception the night before. There were a record six ducks on show and this calamitous defeat would usher in a now infamous sequence of THIRTEEN negative results, culminating in a first ever EGM (more on that later). With the dust having barely settled, Ainsworth's sublime 64 in a T20 at Wootton & Boars Hill would ultimately prove futile, his progress checked by partner Ian Leggate, who this time managed to run somebody else out despite not facing a ball.

One man doth not a team make, though in the case of Chris (Big Bird) Heron, one man *does* make a team. Chris was a strapping, charismatic chap with a jaunty blue cap and sarcastic smile. He plied his boundless batting talents for the Oxford University Press (OUP) and mostly against the FFTMCC, as was the case at the end of May, where he batted all day for 93 not out and won the game singlehandedly. Indeed, such was his aura that Sunday, that if you could bat alone infinatum after everyone else was sat back in their foldaway chairs, then Chris would still be batting today.

Garsington were a new addition to the calendar, another gemstone procured from the OCA league handbook by Ian Howarth. Atop a hill with patchwork fields rolling off into the distance, The MAD set their T20 stall out by thumping 154-5 with Dave Shorten (31* off 14 balls) flexing those builder's shoulders by muscling several balls into nearby Denton. Howarth also enjoyed a short legside boundary before his admirable retirement on 50. Admirable or plain bloody daft was the discussion, after Mr Woodward replied for the hosts with 50 of his own and a further 32 not out on top of that. This entertaining barbarity (for the locals anyway) lasted a mere 13.5 overs and saw fielder Thornton Smith stationed in a wheat field dodging crop sprayers. Calculating GCC's projected run-rate, The MAD would actually have needed to plunder 226 to

† *Another wonderful memory was that of the imposing eating machine Paddy Mellor investing in his seventh or eighteenth hot dog of the day. On deciding to buy two, he returned to his deckchair to hear the tannoy announce "all food [was] now half price." Once again, adjectives used by Patrick can also only be found in the Chambers dictionary.*

Reeves: "Let me introduce you. Wife, drunks – drunks, wife.

have won this game. This midweek dicking also featured one Ralph Anderson Smith from Astons CC, who whilst generously filling a hole in the team, would rebuff club policy by neglecting a Duck on Debut.

Defeats were now coming thick and fast, or shitty and often depending on your particular bent. There was the obligatory misery in Bloxham (Milton away) despite a defiant slog of 30 from beatnik Smith, a T20 pasting at the hands of the local taxi drivers (Marsh XI) and of course another Sunday massacre against Carl McKno's Appleton CC. For several years, MAD shoulders would slope when they spotted Carl on the opposition team sheet. An acerbic northerner of no great height, he ran in as if chasing the bastard who shagged his wife, propelling these unplayable, inswinging yorkers at your soon-to-be splattered stumps. He splattered a few on that day too, with team mates falling apart after watching opener Steve Dobner's wreckage first ball.

Two more T20 reverses were next on the menu. First up was a corporate flogging by Ralph Smith's Centrica XI, before a 10 wicket pummelling at Cutteslowe against near neighbours Isis CC. (Note from the Editor – Ian Howarth has obviously had to reach for the thesaurus on the phrase 'severely beaten' at this point). A sarcastic and timeless report on our website details the disaster in the park, asking players at its end to vote between "Reeves or Westmoreland – who was the shittest?" Both recorded ducks, both dropped sharp chances, but Martin picked up the buffet. I don't know the result of the vote, but imagine it would have been a close run thing. Could it get any worse? You betcha.

The FFTMCC had never beaten the Lemmings, in fact in a decade of trying they had barely come second to this ex-graduate ensemble. Expectations weren't high then for snapping a losing trend, but after reducing the moneyed rodents to 26-3, expectations rose. The MAD soon returned to their default emotion of despair as a combination of

Baker Boys (the team had five family members that day) cudgelled errant bowling all over Brasenose to chalk up 193. A MAD reply would be centred on the bulwark efforts of Howarth, Reeves, Bullock, Leggate and Emerson, who combined faced a total of 12 balls between them in accumulating zero. Howarth was given LBW by Leggate having just woken him from a pissed slumber, before Reeves' magical season hit a new low after copping C. Greenwood's hat-trick ball. It wasn't all bad, Skipper Westmoreland got off the mark and the team managed to bat out their overs in no small debt to Pearson's stoic 60 not out. James' efforts also included an earlier haul of 5-20 and his all -round heroics would be later recognised by Mike Reeves receiving the MOTM award (another protest vote).

With losing becoming an epidemic or not winning a supreme talent, a MAD EGM was invoked so a select panel of 'experts' could better try to understand what was going on. Truth be told, nobody quite knew *what* was going on, other than the website result column reading 'L,L,L,L,L,L,L,L,L,L' and 'L' again (in red ink). Was there any way to reverse this terminal decline? Well, yes actually, as the next opposition were the serially useless Bodleian. A team so poor, that if losing was an art form, they were the Rembrandt of being shit. Meeting adjourned.

Inclement weather, flowing beer and a liberal student gathering formed the backdrop at Mansfield Road for a T20 to decide the shittest team in Oxford (if not the planet). Winning the toss, Skipper Hotson was cheered as his team whacked the bookworms

Howarth before his fateful decision to retire on 50…."

into the vivisection labs before retiring for a pint. A total of 156-6 was surely way in excess of what this dysfunctional librarian collective could even dream about. However, their pathetically humble aspirations were boosted by the hitting of one James Shaw, an altitudinous bespectacled talent who would guest for The MAD later in the year. His 36 retired gave the Bods early impetus (76-2), but as their batsmen, or simply men with a bat, came and went, the innings eventually faltered. But that would be to greatly underestimate The MAD's legendary stupidity. With rain now falling steadily and discussions rife on how *not* to take the last few Bodley rabbits (lest Shaw return), Hotson and Timms' brains backfired. With A. Downey caught and N. Walker run out, it thus ensured James Shaw (49*) *did* return and after pinching the strike, subsequently blazed the first four balls of Westmoreland's final over for victory. The MAD now stood alone in stunned silence having wrestled control of the off-golden T20 Turd Trophy, soaking up the rain and enduring the heckling of a delirious opposition. The drinking continued long after the outcome.

A twelfth consecutive defeat was supplied by the benevolent taxi drivers five days later, a game only remembered because of one player. Coming into this match, Gary Timms' form had seen him plunge down the order after piling up scores of 0,0,4,0,3*,4 and 2 and the only reason he had stopped plunging is because a team only consists of eleven players. If humans were at risk from myxomatosis, then Gary would have had your grave concern. The team consisted of only ten players on this evening and so it was that he joined the indefatigable Dan Edwards at the fall of the eighth wicket. The MAD required just 7 runs to win and in the ensuing panic at seeing Timms at the crease, Edwards ran him out whilst trying to steal back the strike. In a show of great sportsmanship, the Marsh XI called the despondent Timms back and agreed he bat again (as the absent number eleven). Edwards (41*) would then expose his partner just 1 run shy of the opposition total whereby Gary slapped his first ball to the guy in the covers. He thus ended the match by adding a golden duck to his diamond duck and the ignominy of being truly bloody awful.

Jake 'Judge' Hotson overseeing The MAD's world ranking sink lower than the sea bed

There may well have been a clamouring for a TEGM (Total Emergency General Meeting) after four more ducks and defeat against Wootton & Boars Hill, but looming on the horizon was salvation, a T20 versus some touring octogenarians. Perhaps in a show of sarcastic pity, the Saxlingham Gents were recommended to the club by none other than the Bodleian and the sociably rewarding granddads of Norfolk would put up a great fight. Nonetheless, they were to be thanked for bookending the worst sequence in MAD history, a slump of loserdom that lasted only one day shy of two months. For the record, G. J. Timms' drew a blank with his leggies and was run out for 1.

If the FFTMCC thought they'd turned a corner they perhaps had, but in doing so they ran off the road and into a regal ravine. 2011 would mark the last visit to the opulent and breathtaking surrounds of Blenheim Park, thereafter invitations to play on the Duke's lawn fell silent. On a predictably underprepared acreage at the World Heritage Site, The MAD were cock-a-hoop in bowling the hosts out for 86 off 38 tortuous overs. Following teas among the trees on a pasting table (there is no pavilion), Howarth's aerial assault of 47 guided the visitors to 56-3, before he became one of G. Davies' eight eventual victims as the team slid to 59 all out. An utterly bizarre scorecard saw Ian scoring almost 80% of a final total in which the other contributions were scores of 0,3,2,4,0,0,0,0,0 and 0 not out which including Mr Timms being bowled for another golden duck. 7 wickets had fallen for 3 runs and any MAD heartbeat was now a flatline.

With Westmoreland and Hotson looking increasingly forlorn, things thankfully took an upturn before Tour with Wootton & Bladon once again obliging in a record run-chase at Brasenose (I mean how awful were they?) This green 'W' in the website's result column preceded a successful road trip out to Witney to help Paddy Mellor slay his Audley Ducks. They say nobody looks good in their darkest hours, but to see Mike Reeves staggering around under a skier like a village drunk was palpably funereal. Since walking off the Duntisbourne Abbott ground in early May citing 29 as good enough to cement his place at number three, Mike's season had nosedived into the realms of the unthinkable. Other players had been shite, *truly* shite, but at least their aspirations were that. Under the spotlight of sniggering jibes and piss-taking, he had strung together a stellar sequence of knocks which read 3,0,4,0,0,0 (all bowled), 1 LBW, 7 caught, a rare spike of 28 not out (dropped numerous times) followed by 4 and 0 (both bowled). It was *that* bad you held your breath as that ball swirled in the leaden skies, collectively pleading with the cricketing gods to "please, *please* let him catch the bloody thing!" Careers are defined in these moments. The god's took pity that day and Mike's career continued after Witney as he hung on for one of the best MAD team celebrations of the season. He then batted at number three and was LBW for 1, third ball.

Having sat on his indolent backside for *way* too long, organiser James Hoskins simply reversed a home fixture in the end and took the team on tour to Southsea (home of Portchester CC). This vacation was memorable for batting heroics, a toilet seat and not getting your head kicked in by Portsmouth football hooligans. To avoid any bloodletting on the first day, the tourists travelled to Hayling Island where there wasn't

Much to ponder for Mr Timms....

any football and only a couple of angry skinheads. Decked out in pirate gear with an iconic bog seat medallion, Ian Leggate wrote, directed and starred in one of the great FFTMCC matches. Chasing an improbable 229 for victory, The MAD crumbled to 131-8 before Dave Emerson clumped a few to be then caught by a girl. It laid the foundation for a grandstand finish in which Captain Gonzo's defiant and pugnacious efforts (3 not out off 32 balls) just failed to bring the team home (Howarth also played a bit part unbeaten on 109 not out at the other end).

The Hayling Island game included a couple of other memorable moments, including a pre-match pitch inspection of the wrong pitch and the collective chauvinistic terror at the potential of being bowled by Amber Longhurst (a fourteen year old female). T Smith avoided this ignominy, but demonstrated how important it is for a batsman to know where his off stump is. Whilst watched by Howarth at the non-strikers end and Reeves as umpire, he played the most beautiful, fluent, expansive leave as ever seen. Unfortunately the ball was delivered on line, pitched on line and went straight on (on line). Howarth nearly split his hernia and Reeves nearly wet his umpiring trousers.

Saturday was spent avoiding Pompey's 657 Crew, playing pirate golf, getting drunk and feasting off kebab vans before an epic slog of 95 by Emerson on the Sunday. In tandem with Jake Hotson (24*) the pair amassed a MAD record 81 for the eighth wicket at Portchester whilst helping the team post 200-8. In reply, the home team then batted and won. Mr Hoskins' Tour ended with a humping by his brother-in-law's team in Winchester on the way home, but not before The MAD had retrieved the bowling of Mr Leggate from all over the quaint little village of Longparish. Ian's consummate figures of 3-0-62-0 included one twelve ball over getting marmalized for a club record 35 runs. The match also saw the touring introduction of Messrs Pearson and Timms, their day trip seeing James compile a confident 56 whilst Gary compiled another less than confident golden duck.

In lieu of cricketing enthusiasm waning after Tour, Sandra Steinhauer became the fourth female to represent The MAD and the thirty fourth player to join the pantheon of Ducks on Debut. She did however last eight balls longer than Howarth, whose ill-advised sledging of Carl McKno resulted in his exclusive membership of another club, that of the *Platinum*. The obligatory defeat adjacent to Oxfordshire's smelliest sewerage plant was sweetened by Newman-Robson's 4.5-for and a ninth wicket MAD partnership record of 47 between Steve Dobner and James Hoskins. Jon's half a point deduction from his bowling analysis was due to the final victim, Appleton's C. Salmon, hardly qualifying as a junior, let alone an adult.

With team members pinching themselves in disbelief, The MAD somehow won their eighth and ninth games the following week. Howarth's Manhattan skyline of scores continued at Keble College as Pearson helped him add a record 139 for the second wicket against Oxenford. Audibly grumbling throughout this leviathan partnership, Mike Reeves sat impatiently with his pads on. Finally, after 162 balls and major considerations given to alternative sporting pursuits, he walked out to the middle to be caught first ball by substitute 'Tall Bob' Roberts.

A reverse fixture with Portchester at the soulless environs of Horspath Recreational Ground saw the return and final sighting of Aussie gun-for-hire Jenner Collins. For the

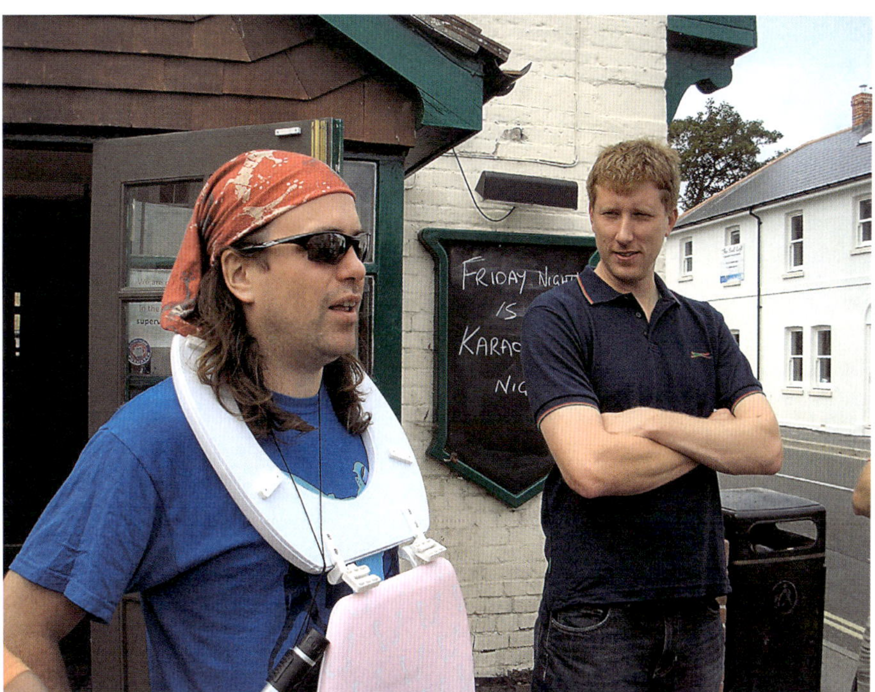

Tall Bob (right) trying to understand Ian Leggate...

second time in less than a month, The MAD once again *just* failed in chasing down 220 plus with the Aussie at his most tonkinglike with a run-a-ball 94. This match was one of three in three days and all but sapped any remaining confidence or team energies. The third match on Sunday witnessed Reeves and Hoskins bowl in tandem from sunrise to sunset, only for the team to then capitulate from 88-4 to 101 all out later in the day. In total, Mike and James bowled unchanged for a record 29 overs at Aston Tirrold, taking eight wickets between them and later being air-lifted to the John Radcliffe to undergo remedial heart surgery.

Another double-header the following weekend saw losing trips to Islip (to play Isis CC) and the fabled Tetsworth. Richard Hadfield made a long awaited return to form on the Saturday, hitting 48 before snapping his hamstring and being declared dead at the scene. His untimely passing followed James Shaw (on debut) going down in the previous over with terminal cramp. It was odd, surreal and maybe this season had well and truly ran its course? But that would be to ignore Sunday's inhospitable battlefield just north of the M40. Harking back to 1916, Captain Westmoreland stood with his loaded bat by a muddied pavilion, knowing full well the situation was hopeless and the sound of a whistle would send his men out to their undoubtable demise. With his pitiful comrades falling all about him, it is to his eternal credit he found the resolve to strike out in a bloodied swamp for his first fifty of the season. Applauded by all who could discern it whilst huddled in the sanctuary of the pavilion, Martin's 59 was followed by a next top score of 9. In what can surely be classed as one his best knocks of the season, Private Reeves somehow avoided predictions, shrapnel and gunfire to finish unbeaten on 5 not out. This was in sharp contrast to Libyan tyrant Muammar Gaddafi, who after surviving French airstrikes that weekend was cornered in a hole.

Finally after twenty one weeks and thirty five matches the guns fell silent on a season lauded as being the pinnacle of shitdom. There had been a record breaking 26 defeats which featured a record breaking 72 ducks of which Gary Timms accounted for more than 11%. Drilling further down into this turd of statistics, a record 22 players contributed to the duck pond of which over 22% were golden (25% of these *also* belonged to Mr Timms). With the Fir Tree on Iffley Road providing a cosy but claustrophobic venue for the AGM, the team pored over a season of non-accomplishment whilst quadrupling the regular bar takings. Jake Hotson was so incensed by his own win loss ratio, he saw fit to auction off the contents of the entire team kit bag and the kit bag itself. On a more positive spin, Howarth scored more runs in a calendar year than anyone had or has since (724 at 34.48 and not meriting any award), whilst Hoskins (38 wickets at 16.29) and Emerson (35 at 17.20) were revelatory with the ball. Dan Edwards chewed up 786 balls hitting 465 runs, whilst the all-round capabilities of James Pearson came into focus with 359 runs at 23.93 coupled with 20 wickets at 17.45. Gary Timms also came into focus, but for very different reasons, failing by one run to match the number of innings he had (15). With Sambuca in charge of the voting, the popularity contest would ultimately be swayed by Dave Emerson's sharp new haircut, pretty-boy looks and his decision to uphold the ethics of the sport by accepting the umpire's decisions (note to self, Ian). In the background, members of the committee buried their heads in their hands and remained in office.

We sometimes need to remind ourselves that cricket is just a game and as the year closed, that premise has never seemed more apt. A wonderful team mate made famous for getting so much right would ultimately and quite devastatingly get something so very wrong. The Far from the MCC would pay homage to Adrian John Fisher whose life was cut short at just forty six and for all those who loved him dear, his passing remains as painful today as it was back then. An imposing character of infinite wit and wisdom, Ade was the ultimate landlord and quizmeister. An indispensable and engaging member of The Jude and The MAD, Glastonbury's celebrated Papa Smurf left an indelible legacy as village cricket's greatest guru of pie. My personal recollections are of a man who always found time to correct my batting, bowling and fielding, before giving counsel on my partying, wardrobe and choice of pub. I look forward to hopefully renewing our bickering one day, somewhere in that great gig in the sky. All the best old mate. ■

Adrian John Fisher (1965-2011). Too well loved to ever be forgotten

MR. TICKLE

2012

Mike Reeves

IN the words of the Cult, "Hot sticky scenes, you know what I mean (no.) Like the desert sun that burns my skin (chance would be a fine thing). I've been waiting for her, for so long, open the skies and let her come down (now we're getting to it.) Here comes the rain, here comes the rain, here she comes again, here comes the rain." Yes 'she' was an all too frequent visitor to the UK and MAD cricket venues in general during 2012. The year 2007 will be forever associated with flooding in Oxfordshire as Mike Reeves developed a temporary swimming pool in his front room, however it was 2012 that saw the greatest havoc reaped on The MAD fixture list. Not a single Sunday game was played throughout the month of June. During this time a familiar pattern emerged as Captain Westmoreland (Moo) would have to ring around on a Sunday morning to deliver the sad but inevitable news that another afternoon had been lost. In many cases it was a blessed relief as dispiriting trips to in-laws or garden centres had already been organised in anticipation.

When the team weren't playing matches due to the weather, they weren't playing them because our home ground of Brasenose was either underwater or out of action due to vandalism. A particularly rowdy wedding in the pavilion had seen several glasses smashed and fragments making their way on to the pitch.

The year had started predictably enough with the now annual dicking against Horspath, a match noteworthy only for a spirited first day performance from Steve Dobner (42). Oh, how the summer must have seemed so bright and welcoming to him at that point.

Game two was the annual trip to Wootton & Bladon. Close your eyes and picture the scene of a beautiful English cricket ground, a wonderful thatched pavilion is separated from the closely mown outfield by a white picket fence. Deckchairs surround the boundary rope on a gently rising slope which forms a natural amphitheatre as the dappled light is cast across the ground through a row of mature oak trees. Now open your eyes and see that W&B is none of these things. It's a windswept field barely given over from football or strip grazing. There is no pavilion, meaning that players must

Brasenose staged the annual Oxford Carp Fishing Contest in 2012.

hump their kit from the local(ish) school across the road to deposit it in the middle of nowhere.

So what makes a good cricket ground? Number one is not having the local 'yoof' riding around the outfield on mopeds, or adjacent to a graffiti splattered boundary wall with 'terror.ism' scrawled on it. For these reasons, Cowley Marsh municipal ground is probably the worst we've ever played on, although by 2012 we had long dispensed with its services. The next crucial element is the proximity of the pavilion to the pitch. Somewhere for the scorers to sit and the batting side to congregate is important and therefore the aforementioned W&B, along with Stratfield Brake, Horspath municipal pitch and possibly even Enstone fall in to a lower category, where captains have to cajole players in to making the trip. The ground being used exclusively for cricket is perhaps the next defining feature, so huge arenas such as Astons (although they score heavily in the being next door to Tim Henman category) and Harwell lose marks here.

Next we come to grounds which are a pleasure to play on. I like Appleton (so long as the wind isn't blowing from the sewage works end), Wootton & Boars Hill, and Cholsey now at their new home. Into this category come many of the college pitches such as Jesus College and our neighbours (Isis CC) at Queens College, which most agree just pips our own beloved Brasenose (it has a bar for one thing and showers which weren't built for six year olds). Finally, top of the shop are those grounds which encapsulate everything that is loved about English cricket. These are the grounds where players who haven't made the teamsheet will turn up along with other spectators, just to sample the atmosphere. We all have a special appreciation of Pylewell in Lymington, but there's also grounds like Cumnor, where the pavilion sits well above the field and provides a gorgeous natural setting.

You'll notice that I've given very small consideration to the quality of the playing surface itself. Other than the obvious horror of playing on an artificial surface (see Mansfield Road, Wytham and horror of horrors, right up there with Cowley Marshes now that I think of it, Holton), so long as it's not actually dangerous (see Cholsey's old ground) then whether the ball keeps low or bounces true is of relatively little consequence at this level.

Into the desolation of W&B stepped two men to define that day. One was Ian Leggate, who had decided the icy wastes of Canada were preferable to an English summer and was thus playing his last match for quite some time. The other was Chris Roberts (career average 5.2) who smashed 11 off 6 balls to see The MAD win by one wicket with two balls to spare. His stirring boundary to seal the win was a certainty for Champagne moment, but would subsequently also scoop the Champagne moment of the season. Take it where you can get it Bob, days like these don't come along very often for many of us, as was ably demonstrated in the next game, a T20 against Garsington.

The match occurred on 22nd May and at this point of the season we would normally have expected to have played 9 or 10 games, but the report of that time was quick to point out that a lack of sunshine was already a regular occurrence. The MAD had reached one of their low points in losing by 47 runs, with extras to thank for a top score of 27. A club record three golden ducks in an innings included Nick Hebbes' suicidal

A fond farewell to the Legend of Leggate

run out first ball. The only boundary for our team came in the 18th over from the blade of Gary Timms, our number 11 and therefore a certainty for another Champagne moment (or Warm Cava moment as it is sometime called in these situations). However, sometimes the horseshit of a performance provides rich manure for the shoots of recovery, leading to a seedling of bright future and so was the case here. This match provided a debut for one Russell Paul Turner.

Russell, Russ, Homer (because of his now legendary tea eating prowess), Mystic (because he once claimed to have a secret method of predicting coin tosses) or latterly Mike Ashley (his doppelganger of Sports Direct fame) quickly became a club regular and stalwart, once it was established that he had access to a printing press and could therefore produce free fixture cards and a second rate cricket book. Russ can be described as a 'sweeper upper', a guy who will volunteer for the jobs which are a logistical pain. Need a captain when the regular captain, T20 captain or first and second vice captains are unavailable? Russ will step in. Need someone to collect the cash when the treasurer is AWOL? Russ is your man. Always jovial, always cordial and with a self-effacing sense of humour to go with a steadying influence around number four, Russ we salute you.

The very next game (customary and otherwise un-noteworthy annual defeat to Milton CC away) saw the debut of Johannes van den Grootschnyke Webster, Jan to his friends.

Nick Hill, purveyor of the classic cover drive

His origins are slightly unclear, although he claims he was once perusing a second-hand bookshop and came across of copy of 'Not at This Level', The MAD's vastly superior prequel to this tome. He was so inspired by the words of Antony Mann, that he immediately made it his life's ambition to be part of the team. Alternatively it could have been that he was something to do with regular opponent OUPCC. Despite his relatively modest number of appearances, Jan is one of those guys who just seems to belong in the team. As in cricket, as in life, there are some people who are comfy in their own skin and just seem to fit in. So if you're a slightly eccentric bookworm from a minor European cricket playing nation, with possibly some obscure connection with other teams in Oxfordshire, do get in touch, you'll fit right in.

2012 also saw the arrival of the fresh faced Brummie, Nick Hill, our first T20 specialist and a guy with one of the shortest names in MAD history. His true calling was for baseball and he did try, with limited success, to adapt those skills to the cricket pitch. A typical innings from Nick would be out (bowled) for 4 off 2 balls.

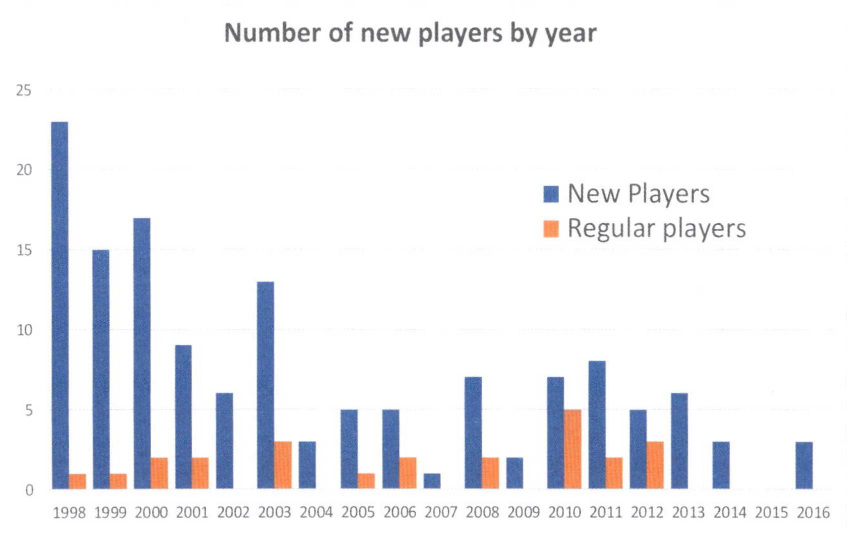

The inclusion of Russ, Jan and Nick meant that from 2012 onwards the team was pretty much complete. The chart above shows the number of players who have debuted in each year since 1998. Also shown is the number of those players who still, as of 2017, are club regulars. So we can see for example that in 1998, 23 players debuted for the club, of whom only one, Matt Bullock, is still a club regular.

So, can the team be divided into three distinct groups? The Founders, who have been around forever, The Saviours, who joined in 2003 when the club looked like folding, and The Centrica Lot, who followed Dave Emerson around 2010. Also, what does it tell us about the future of the team? No new players since 2012 means that we're now a closely knit unit, but with none of us getting any younger it might feel like there is a limited lifespan for the club as decrepitude sets in. Certainly it's becoming increasingly difficult for new players to join the team and find enjoyment, what with all the in-jokes and banter which goes with such a long shared knowledge of matches. In fact, the experience of our club seems to match that of many of the teams we play. The same old (and older) faces turning up each year means that the vast majority of players now 'get it' leading to pleasant Sunday cricket, but you have to wonder whether we are a dying breed....

June started brightly with a Friday evening encounter against a Centrica (British Gas) XI. With The MAD somehow retaining the services of Dave Emerson and James Pearson, the opposition was full of Judas's, including Ralph Smith, Rob Eaglestone, Nick Hill, Lee Ainsworth and the Judiest of Judas's, one Mr G. J. Timms. Gary shone with the bat like he never did for The MAD, scoring 29 including three fours and a six (doesn't count for your average though, Gaz). He also took two wickets and affected a direct run out, all of which had regular MAD skipper Mr Westmoreland scratching his head and wondering where the hell the real Gary Timms had vanished to.

With so little cricket going on, there was a bountiful opportunity to get the literary juices flowing and pour your heart and soul into a website match report. So that would be less of the actual playing cricket and more of the actual writing about it. A proud history of trying to find the offbeat elements of matches stretches all the way back to Antony Mann and latterly continued by the likes of Nick Hebbes, Ian Howarth and Mike Reeves. Basically, you take an obscure facet of the game, or even something not related to the game at all and expand it into the centrepiece of the report itself. A particularly fine example of this is the report from Ian Howarth, detailing the T20 encounter between FFTMCC and OU Offices at the end of June. Built entirely around an imaginary 5-Live commentary, it is a classic of the genre. Incidentally, The MAD won that game on the last ball of the match after Brasenose has finally been discovered at the top of Mount Ararat.

2012 will be remembered for the only day all summer that the sun shone properly . The 22nd of July was utterly glorious. Players and spectators alike donned their beachwear, café societies sprang up and hosepipe bans were in effect. It was also the day that Martin Westmoreland played what was to become his now trademark one good innings of the year. His 75, along with able support from Steve Dobner and of course extras, posted an imposing total of 209 for Cholsey to chase. Timms, Roberts, Emerson and Dobner all cashed in as the visitors collapsed, providing a thumping 137 run win. One sided matches such as this aren't always the best and in future years Cholsey would provide much sterner tests, but for just this one day it was beautiful. The match report was based around the exploits of James Hoskins, who had been a mainstay of the club and led the team in terms of wickets and matches played. In 2012 he took a year off to take a bus halfway around the world on some sort of a photographic pilgrimage, taking in potholing, ballooning, eating arachnids and courting his fiancée Polly Moon (see chapter 2017). He picked a good year to go, but still, going from an ever present to a never present was felt by everyone throughout the year.

Against a backdrop of the London Olympics around the end of July, The MAD recorded close wins against new opponents Harwell and more familiar foes St Clements Strollers. A highlight of the former game was Dan Edwards being out for a Platinum duck (i.e. first ball of the match) resulting in Number 3, Ian Howarth being summoned mid-dump from the toilet to go out and bat. The latter game again featured Dan, but this time in more positive light as he provided a match winning partnership with ex-Marlborough House colleague Mike Reeves, as they posted a total marginally beyond the Strollers on the picturesque Magdalen College ground. By the way, for those of you unfamiliar with Oxford, Magdalen is pronounced Mauldin. Only an idiot would think that it's pronounced phonetically, Mag-da-lein.

Thus to Tour and talking of only idiots thinking that places are pronounced phonetically, Patrick Mellor still insists that our first opponents Happisburgh are pronounced Hap-is-berg, whereas Mike Reeves knows that they are correctly known as Hays-borough. Mike has experience of the area, having designed the beach defences to stop East Norfolk disappearing into the sea, so it's a wonder that there's any of it left, no matter how it's pronounced.

Evidence of the one day of sunshine in 2012

Tour organiser that year was Dave Emerson, who secured lodgings near one of the UK's more (in)famous seafronts by typing into Google 'very cheap B&B, Great Yarmouth', and subsequently accepting the first thing on the list. Thus it was that most of the team rocked up at the Trevross Hotel, to be greeted by the hosts, presumably Trevor and Rosalind. When it's said 'most of the team' this is of course with the exception of Jake Hotson, who in what is now part and parcel of tour classics, spent the first night sleeping on a bench outside because of being locked out. Come the morning and one of his teammates showed him that he hadn't in fact been 'locked out', but had simply failed to grasp the difference between 'push' and 'pull' when it comes to opening doors.

Prior to the first match against Happisburgh (Hays-borough) the team congregated at a lovely pub just moments from the ground. It was subsequently to everyone's consternation that following the game, we drove miles to a Harvester type pub where Patrick Mellor acted as fines chairman to deliver a blistering, eye watering fines total of £126.50, which is a club record unlikely ever to be beaten.

Mike Reeves was captain of the team that day. He has a short and not too admirable history of skippering the team, being deficient in the essential skills of tactics and man management. He is still scarred from the experience of the entire team wanting to bat at number six during the tour of Louth. Dan Edwards approached Mike to announce that he would like to open the batting, to which Mike replied with the now infamous phrase

Shooting Gallery as organised by Saxlingham Gents

"good for you". Dan assumed that a slot at either one or two (his choice obviously) was now nailed on and he duly appeared fully padded up, five minutes before the start of the game, this before Mike informed him that number eight had been specially reserved for him. Mike never captained the team again, Dan hardly played ever again and the two have barely spoken since. On the up-side the phrase "good for you" has now passed in to folklore and is enshrined in the Glossary section of the website. The tin hat was put on Mike's day when he developed a severe allergic reaction to a combination of plants, beer and his teammates at the pub that evening, causing his entire body to turn scarlet. The sensible thing to do in this situation would have been to take him to A&E, but that would have cut down on drinking time, so he was left to his own devices and it was all fine by the morning.

The second game of tour was against the ageing Saxlingham Gents, who had snapped The MAD's longest ever losing streak the season before (13 games). Following Ian Howarth's paying of a king's ransom to secure a coach for the day, the bus toured Norfolk for most of the afternoon whilst failing to find a single open pub. Later Patrick Mellor revealed he was descended from a long line of commercial transport owning Norfolkites and could have furnished the team for a pauper's paycheque. Howarth would go on to skipper the team and brought an interesting new twist to the batting line up, where the order was dictated by height and then a coin toss to decide the orientation (Tall Bob could be batsman Number 1 or Number 11). A thoroughly good-natured game notable for Steve Dobner (35) returning from enforced retirement to run himself out, The MAD weren't overly disappointed to lose by a single run. The team returned to Oxfordshire after the third game, a thorough mangling at the hands of Marlingford at their leafy, picturesque little ground adorned with Olympic Union Jack bunting. Despite three defeats, one near death by asphyxia, one night on a park bench, several severe hangovers, some bed bugs and a haemorrhaging of cash on fines and coach fares, it had been another wonderfully successful tour.

By some miracle (and an unbeaten 65* from Dan Edwards who batted all day), the team managed to shake off the traditional post tour hangover by winning their next game away at Appleton. The following weekend, The MAD were invited to the Jesus and Lincoln college grounds for their first T20 tournament. It looked a strong line-up and on paper we appeared to be the weakest of the four teams invited, however in the first game against Oxenford CC, thanks to Howarth, Edwards and Pearson, we posted a fairly respectable 121-5. In reply Oxenford scored 120 for 7 in 19.5 overs and therefore Captain Westmoreland judged that so long as one run or less was conceded, we would be through to the final. He duly pushed the field back and conceded just the one run. The FFTMCC walked off to imaginary applause and a place in the final until an obscure (or possibly immediately invited) rule in the event of a tie was invoked, we would have to play a 'super over'. That didn't go so well, with Oxenford scoring 8 in their over whilst in reply Howarth, Emerson and Westmoreland managed a single. A slightly disgruntled MAD team would have to duke it out in the wooden spoon contest. This third placed playoff took place at the adjacent Lincoln College and despite the long

Duck turns his back on abject failure

winded description of what makes a good cricket ground (detailed earlier), the pitch was a dog and the game never really got going. There was a collective feeling of not being bothered and the team sunk to a seven wicket loss.

Despite the losses, the Oxenford game will be remembered chiefly for two heroic efforts with the ball, Chris Roberts and Dave Emerson taking four and three wickets respectively. Bob's performance in particular, which included three wickets in the final over to tie the game (all bowled), would scoop him the inaugural presentation of the Adie Fisher trophy, an accolade for the stand out single performance of the season named in honour of our sadly departed teammate. For Emerson, it was just one of a number of stellar contributions which would go on to earn him the Player of the Season award for the second year running (302 runs at 16.78 and 18 wickets at 20.11).

It was now the tail end of the season and in a double header, The MAD hosted a touring Portsmouth team on the Saturday. Martin Westmoreland played his second, once in a season, super innings but despite this the touring side were way too strong. I remember this game on the artificial strip at Mansfield Road for getting hit for the biggest six I have ever seen. Back over my head, it cleared the 30 foot fence beyond the boundary and was irretrievable from the pitch next door. Others may remember the debilitated state of Paul Hungerford, whose Birthday falls on tour each year, the ailing Portchester keeper asleep in his own vomit on his kit bag.

The penultimate game of the season was against The Astons, a game remembered for several incidents. Firstly, a wonderful 102 not out from Ralph Smith, who along with his de facto sidekick John Shea, helped post an impressive 217-5. During the innings, a ball went flying towards the pavilion, bouncing off the hand rail in front of the spectators and straight in to Tony Mander's head. Fortunately there was a doctor in the house, unfortunately it was Tony. If we were going to chase down such a total then everyone was going to have to fire on all cylinders, especially our in-form skipper Moo, coming off his rousing 89 just the day before. However, unfortunately, he was triggered run out for just one by the home team umpire. Still, an honest mistake I'm sure, but after that bungled adjudication, the life drained out The MAD reply and we slumped to a sizeable defeat.

All that remained was a lacklustre seven wicket defeat to the Isis in which five players each scored five, and the team not being arsed with a friendly knock about thereafter. Ian Howarth signed off the match report by saying, "There have been highs, there have been lows and in fact there have been some subterranean lows, but as always we take amusing memories with us. We look forward in earnest to a far drier 2013." ■

Far from the MCC
109

2013

Ian Howarth

HBO's 'The Wire' ran for five seasons and is universally regarded as one of the greatest dramatisations of all time. The Far from the MCC would beg to differ, as anyone who worked on stage or behind the scenes would advocate 'The Westmoreland Years' as a far better work. It had an equally ingenious script, but blessed with a comedian's sleight of hand interwoven with masterful small-scale characters. The Wire just finished, but TWY will always be remembered for its mind-bogglingly inventive finale, one which would utterly implausible if it were not based on fact (but more on that later).

Despite the unrelenting misery of a northern Jetstream which decided on being southerly and crapping all over Oxfordshire for much of 2012, Martin Westmoreland pulled on the Captain's shit-absorption suit and rallied himself for "one more year". This was it, the final push from a guy who had donated an eighth of his life to contacting recalcitrant teammates, changing their nappies and dealing with Sunday cricket's biggest headache which is placating everyone whilst trying to win. Martin's is now regarded as a truly herculean effort of shit-management on a truly cosmic sporting scale.

The start of the season was cold, but it always is, even if it's warm. Everything is alien after a winter under the duvet or down the pub, although watching Horspath slip through the gears and batter up a billion runs wasn't and nor was watching Dan Edwards with a bat in his hands under a large brimmed bat. He'd switched codes you see, gone from the cosy embrace of a bunch of lads on the piss to that other environment where you stamp on someone's throat in the name of winning league points. Most people do it in reverse, but Dan always did tread a path less worn. He batted at seven that day and probably faced as many balls, but he always could turn to his bowling and that legendary octopus threshing around in a washing machine took 3-4 as his old teammates were shot out for 51. Bastard. Life after Dan Edwards was never going to be an easy. Somebody else had to step up and chew through a hundred balls, pinch a single off the fifth or sixth ball and stand in the slips all day with their hands in their pockets. Candidates weren't exactly forthcoming, although several of the guys seemed adept at standing around with their hands in their pockets.

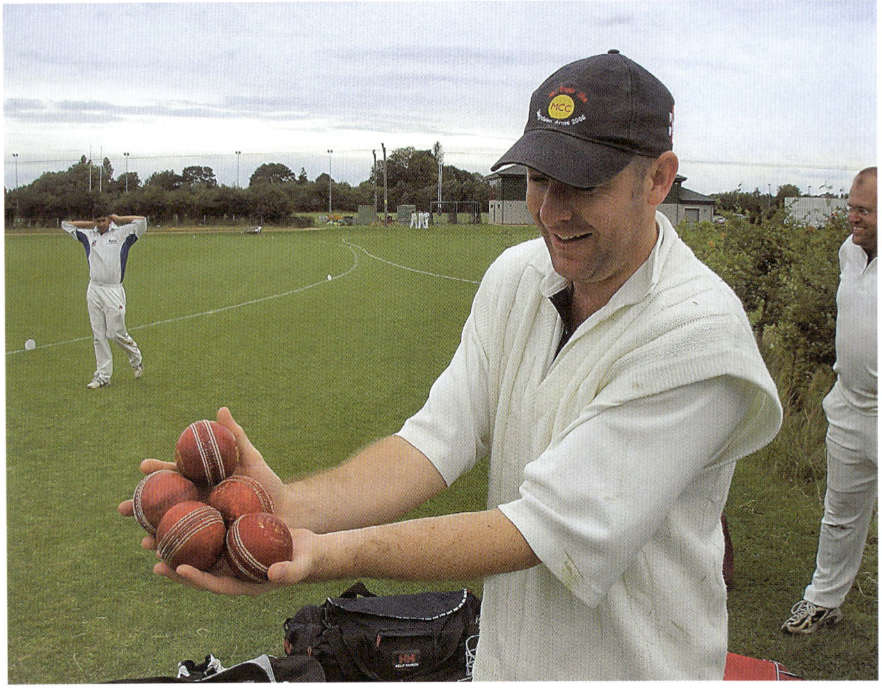

The longest suffering skipper in MAD history (thus far)

A naturalised replacement for the god fearing gardener perhaps came in Germanic form. After watching Turner, Pearson and Westmoreland waste 17 balls in accounting for nothing, Adam Samuel Ward strode to a Wootton & Boars Hill wicket to ably demonstrate all the defensive techniques the above personnel had not. Blue eyed and handsome, brown hair refuted any Arian talk, but Adam instantly replaced Father Darley and Diamond Dave as the new face for club merchandising. His stoic partnership of 82 with Steve Dobner was ultimately in vain, however The MAD did bat their overs out and Gary Timms did make double figures (15*). Sadly, the lure of higher corporate bucks would see Adam leave his colleagues at Centrica and also those at his new found club. He also turned his back on the life of an eligible bachelor too, marrying the undoubtedly gorgeous Charlotte. The one thing he never turned his back on was David Emerson's bat, an item still believed in his possession along with his current address.

Enstone became a new fixture in the FFTMCC calendar and a new place to die of hypothermia. Situated in north Oxfordshire, but always feeling like Estonia, Geoff Carter had his works van stolen a few years ago and slammed into their pavilion. Not sure how much money was stolen, but the bandits probably enjoyed the cheap beer on tap. The ground has a decent artificial strip and players are expected to wear plimsolls to complement their arctic fleeces which fit snugly over their jumper and hoodie. After umpire Timms ensured Westmoreland's miserable start to the season continued, The MAD's aforementioned OAP (Carter) developed acute schizophrenia by batting with the kind of urgency not seen since the police contacted him regarding the pavilion. His 39 remains his greatest score and is the benchmark by which all ageing has-beens aspire to. Regardless, the hosting Eskimos chased down the 174-8 despite Westmoreland's colourful 4-for-plenty.

An amusing sub-story to this arctic misadventure was that belonging to Mark Rundle. Coming into this match after making his debut back in 2011, the self-styled Psycho was now in striking distance of Westmoreland's legendary unwanted record of most successive overs without a wicket. He knew it, the team knew it and after negotiating 4.3 overs of military dross, Enstone's batsmen did too, as Mr Rundle bathed in the adulation of achieving cricket's equivalent of the bowling menopause. The wicket would finally come in Mark's thirty sixth over, 617 days since this sequence of ineptitude first commenced.

With UKIP performing unexpectedly well in local elections, the FFTMCC were performing unexpectedly well in Oxfordshire and Swindon. An unbeaten partnership of 78 in distant Wanborough saw Reeves (48*) rediscover some form aided by Geoff Carter's other-self who can apparently bat. Earlier, bowling spitfires Emerson and Newman-Robson had swung the ball so much that seventeen wides had complemented their complete unplayability. That or the batting was as shit as the keeping. Salad would go on to steal the headlines a fortnight later too, following an historic four-trick which saw a Heron-less OUP detonate from 22-1 to 22-5. FOUR superb wickets in FOUR

Mr Ward using his own bat

mesmeric balls. This legendary ninth over would ensure Howarth's run-a-ball 77 in a sixth highest MAD total ever (222) became forgotten memories. Another justification for those that consider it a bowler's game anyway.

After a pissed congregation at the previous year's AGM seemingly forgot a committee directive to fast-track Gary Timms to the T20 captaincy, Jake Hotson had been installed for a deserved third season as T20 Godfather. Subsequent discussions behind a toilet door meant he was unceremoniously dumped some five minutes later. Credit where credit is due, Jake didn't once question democracy or call the committee "a bunch of c____." So it was that Timms would oversee victories against Blewbury and the Gas Conglomerate, but his stripes were well and truly earned a week previous in one of the most dramatic and damaging matches *ever* played.

A wonderful report on The MAD website lampoons a quite wretched day in Woodstock, where only the name itself evoked anything like the spirit of that seminal festival of yore. In weather that started shit and finished worse, all those who participated in this reduced 20 over farce remain scarred to this day. It is hard to emphasise the sheer misery of a day where bowling and fielding in freezing rain was a harbinger to batting in a blitzkrieg of mud. The ramifications are pertinent to this day. The miserable photo of Derek Hambridge shivering under Timms' rainbow umbrella as his scorebook turned to slush should ensure we never *ever* start a game of cricket in the rain again. Oh, and we lost.

A happier T20 was the one where the Bodleian showed up at Jesus College and we gave them a good five wicket spanking. Beating the Bodleian wouldn't normally merit a bulletin, let alone a mention in this book, unlike losing to them of course, but this game

Never, never, ever, ever, ever again....

was different as is marked James Hoskins' 200th wicket for The MAD. An awesome achievement for someone who gallops up to the wicket off two paces and lobs some rudimentary flan. James' milestone was even more notable for the fact his 199th wicket had occurred some 636 days previously. However this wasn't a barren spell of biblical, side-splitting proportions such as that experienced by Mark Rundle, it was due to an enforced exile of self-discovery and romance after he left his teammates in the lurch to go globetrotting. We've always believed our Club to be one the friendliest and welcoming, so after JMO ran out of money and rocked up in his mum's clapped out Peugeot, after all that time flying hot air balloons, scrambling about potholes, eating spiders and being down with Buddha, he was wholeheartedly accepted back into the fold to buy his own beers.

We now turn to the dark art to coin tossing. If there is such a thing as a soothsayer or a genuine mystic Meg, then they have never captained The MAD. We can certainly discount potential claimants Westmoreland and Timms or their deputies Turner and Emerson. In a quite staggering sequence of bunglability they contrived to lose 19 of 22 coin tosses from 28th April to 24th July, which meant 86.36% of the opposition got to do exactly what they wanted on and between those dates.

Whilst midweek successes were in stark contrast to the shitty coin tossing, Sunday results were not. The MAD's bread and butter was going stale. Pearson's stoic 66 was not enough to spare a drubbing off Islamic State (Isis CC) and Russ Turner's supervisory debut versus St Clements was no different. In the latter game, pieman J Finch somehow took 7-11 off 4.5 overs with his off breaks (or slow nothingy short crust) after D Wiskin got bored after smashing fourteen boundaries. Damian is well known to the club, being that dry and full faced pastiche of everything villagey who diligently divides his time as groundsman, serial beater of The MAD and experienced local pisshead. His 70 here came at a rate of knots not recorded, but probably not many, followed by a comedic retirement as laughable as it was disdainful. One day Mr Wiskin, one day....

Much akin to a gobby drunk staggering outside a Glasgow pub, the Lemmings encounter has always presented itself as the perfect stage for the FFTMCC to showcase their sponge-like ability to absorb a good shoeing. 2013 was no different, only it was, as this time the Oxford intellectuals had pulled an additional ace out the Uni pack with the inclusion of former Wisden Cricketer of the Year and England cricket captain, Claire Taylor. No stranger to the menfolk of The MAD, having salsa danced with Mr Leggate four years previous, Claire was given an opportunity to batter us around Brasenose to the delight of her entourage. This she did for a while, before giving Chairman Matt Bullock a reason to have the scorecard laminated and displayed on his mantelpiece with a line which read:

S. C. Taylor MBE+ c Bullock b Lawrence 22.

Role reversal – Claire keeping with Bullock on strike

By this midway point in the season, absentees, injuries and holidays had stripped The MAD cupboard bare. It was so bad that rather than make up numbers with a stuffed mallard and his two young boys, Captain Westmoreland joined the rest of the team in the knackers' yard. Henceforth, it was Russ Turner now shouldering the grief and monotony of weekend defeats and handing debuts to Steve Lawrence, Rahman Alizha and Stuart Ackland. Steve (OUP) and Stuart (Bodleian) had kindly freed up their Sundays, whilst Mr Alizha was simply glad to be out of his kebab shop on the Cowley Road.

Rahman would star in one of the few bright spots in June at Harwell, whacking 33 runs from a bat discarded by Chris Roberts because it had "no middle". He demonstrated admirable ignorance of building an innings and his mini-cyclone of thrashing was befitting of someone inhabiting a completely different universe to the rest of us. It also tipped the game in our favour. Thereafter it was Milton away (shite), Enstone at home (shite) and Astons at home (totally shite). The Astons game had actually been reversed to Aston Tirrold for reasons I can no longer remember, but imagine the issue was with our groundsman getting battered on the Cowley Road and being unable to raise himself to mow the wicket. Regardless, the outcome was still negative, but at least it saw the return of the injured Westmoreland (30) helping Turner (48*) to bat out the day. This after an early collapse encouraging Howarth to detail a match report based on the plant life he discovered whilst circling the boundary.

But away from the understaffed weekend maulings and US whistleblower Edward Snowden's leaking of NSA files, how was Mr Timms getting on? Well, Gary was quietly and efficiently losing every toss, bullying the Bodleian masochists and earning his stripes whilst ensuring The MAD remained mostly competitive. Blewbury & Upton were new opposition, shunning LBW at home whilst playing *proper* cricket on the road. Ignoring the laws of governance is one thing, but ignoring your stumps is another altogether, with Dave Shorten bypassing any pads with figures of 3-2-4-4. A picturesque college ground is of obvious appeal to league players as the BUCC who landed at Brasenose a few weeks later was unrecognisable. Gone were the kids and shuffling paunch, for here a combative, muscular beast held sway. The beast was Barrett, James and John, and these most eligible bachelors took aim. Emerson (4-0-40-1) copped the main salvo as 29 balls bowled to the brothers equated to 69 runs.

One amusing evening soiree concerned the visit of Appleton CC. Regarded as perennial opposition and containing a host of a familiar faces, some of the friendships are even genuine. On a pitch of rare bounce the visitors made 109-4 and with McKno absent on stump smashing duties elsewhere, The MAD swaggered to 71-1 after 11 overs. Those of a mathematical disposition would instantly realise this game as unloseable. However those of a mathematical disposition with a baccalaureate in advanced FFTMCC calculus would not. Russ Turner had barely retired into the smug confines of his deckchair, before he was padding up again after watching eight wickets fall in as many overs (all bowled). Chest puffed out, he joined Mr Hadfield at the crease who despite yet *another* hamstring tear and enforced amputation, stood firm. Cajoling Richard's corpse as they stuttered to 102-9, Turner then marmelised a pie off C. Jones for the winning runs, or at least he would have if he hadn't found Martin Bungay pissing himself on the deep mid-wicket boundary. In conclusion, this match found ample space on the crowded pantheon of MAD cricketing incompetence.

With Tour now looming on the horizon it was important to rekindle some form in the longer format of the game. That said, 35 or 40 overs can often seem immaterial, as was the case at Brasenose against Wootton & Bladon where we were unreservedly shit in being shot out for 77. Mercifully, Wootton were equally as clueless, however they are lucky enough to possess a batsman cum wicketkeeper who defies cricketing logic. With a dozen rolls of black sticky tape holding his tree trunk together, Gary Doggett hobbles to the crease like a man who has barely survived a car crash. Looking like an extra from Deliverance, he'll fumble and mumble for a few balls, before crunching anything around a length in an arc over the bowlers head. It is an exquisite cocktail of raw power and a wonderful eye, being both utterly perplexing and almost impossible to bowl to.

Mr Doggett minding the stumps

That was the case here as he hauled Wootton over the finishing line in his dusty old pickup truck with 39 not out.

Before setting sail for Weston-super-Mare, Emerson's elder brother, Danial, guested for the club in the return against Harwell. Balder than Dave because he had no hair, Danial had a disentranced aura about him that suggested some shitty Invercargill primary school accounted for his last experience of the game. He certainly fielded like it in his red slippers, and he certainly batted like it during his eight ball duck, but he could undeniably bowl. Perhaps because of his comedic efforts in the lead up, his haul of 2-30 off 7 overs was all the more impressive. A depleted FFTMCC under Howarth should not have worried however, as his brother slammed 48 from the outset and James Pearson did what James Pearson does, which is simply to bat all day (124 balls for 64* being the second longest innings in MAD history and the second most successful in terms of a cure for insomnia).

As fate would have it the BBC's One Show were broadcasting live during The MAD's tour of Weston. Not that any of the team gave a shit about the gooey liberal nonsense that is Matt Baker, but being able to ogle Alex Jones on a sunny beach in all her lovely yellow finery was divine. Throw in a Wetherspoon's beer garden on the seafront for less than £2.50 a pint and Jake Hotson's organisational acumen was to become truly respected. A drunken T20 loss to the town's cricket club allowed Howarth to whack a

Rundle (left) ensuring his trainers are clean of shit

shitfaced 48 as a precursor to the addled bowling heroics of Bullock (2-16) and Mellor (1-14). Always the benevolent, James Hoskins' was busy subsiding Tour on the back of his cricket themed nags, whilst never once whinging about his place in the batting order. Further losses were memorable for Westmoreland (71) returning to the Wembden dugout looking like a battered boxer after withstanding a left-arm barrage from a banned B. Pope, and Paddy Mellor's humping of Dave Emerson all over Somerset after opening the batting for Belvedere. Tour is never without scandal of course and the best was saved for the final day, after the proprietors of the Corbiere B&B informed their guests at breakfast that someone had trudged dogshit up the staircase. The trail spiralled all the way up, with each ninety degree turn giving way to an artistic brushstroke of turd, past Emerson's seedy single and finally onto the joint boudoir of Messrs Howarth and Rundle. 'Shitgate' would be solved by Mark noting Ian's bare feet and absence of any trainers.

As Egypt slowly descended into an unruly mess of civil chaos and massacres, Dave Emerson guided a crack S16 squad to victory against the OUP. In a tense finale in near darkness in the absence of a soon-to-be hitched Mr Timms, Jake Hotson remembered to turn up with his miner's helmet and star with the bat at number eleven. Pearson also starred by becoming the first MAD batsman to be stumped first ball, but not the first to be labelled a cock.

A chastening season looked to be ending as it had started, with lamentable weekend batting displays against Appleton and Oxenford which saw no fewer than eight ducks. There were a few slivers of happiness though, Timms and Rundle adding 51 by the sewerage plant to claim The MAD's highest tenth wicket partnership and the Emerson Bros shining with both bat and ball in a four wicket reverse in Aston Tirrold. Actually Danial didn't bat, so perhaps that is why he shone?

It was raining and miserable on the 8th of September. It was the final game of the season and with family commitments taking precedent, it was also Martin Westmoreland's final match in charge. The setting was Geoff Carter's previous pastime in Cassington, a delicious pudding of a ground already given up to footballing chavs and snarling pit bulls. The shitty weather would finally relent, allowing some plastic train fencing to be deployed as a shield to the crèche / pavilion and twenty two unenthusiastic grumbling males to enter the ring. Martin's dream finale was quickly extinguished as he edged behind, but Howarth (60) and Carter (28) somehow forged on amongst the clumps of long grass and mud. 150 certainly looked a competitive total and as Isis slipped to 99-6, victory was in the bag. But that would be to ignore MAD and Jude history where the needle of defeat can always be located in the shit haystack. However, in losing no further wickets, Isis had seen their overs swallowed up, to which end they still needed three to win off the final ball, or two for a draw. Those of gifted numeracy would swiftly note a dot or single would be insufficient and therefore equate to a MAD win. But if you're thick and still reading this, the permutations are now printed above.

Talking shit – Geoff and Howarth (nearest)

With fielders patrolling the boundary the final delivery needed to be pitched up. Worst case scenario, prevent defeat and concede a draw. As it was, Howarth dragged it short down leg allowing Nick Wyatt to swivel and thrash it behind square. Luckily Roberts and Smith were lurking in the deep, however unluckily Morecambe saw fit to tee it up for Wise who volleyed it over the line. With heads sinking into hands and the air discoloured purple, Carter was busy celebrating behind the stumps. Was this silly old bastard a turncoat or had he finally lost his grip on reality? Inexplicably, Mr Wyatt had stepped on his stumps whilst delivering the final blow, thus out hit wicket. A remarkable curtain call to end Martin's five seasons at the helm and the first victory over Isis CC at the fourteenth attempt.

Thirty players represented the FFTMCC over the course of the season, with a creaking Dave Emerson (30 wickets from 147.1 overs at 17.33) holding Westmoreland

Bez / Hugo – take your pick

responsible for flogging him the most. Howarth (517) and Turner (370) topped the runs aggregate, whilst a resurgent Mike Reeves scooped the Player of the Season award with 269 runs at 24.45 to complement his 27 wickets at 14.07. Gary Timms announced himself with 30 wickets at 19.00 and only four ducks accrued. Another player to debut in a season of lean resources was the aftershave sponsored Hugo Scott, a technically correct batsman in a pork pie hat who perhaps wasn't technically correct in knowing Summertown's party animal, Ian Leggate. Hugo had that imponderable post-rave aura about him, staring off into the distance as if a dawn sun was ushering in a whole new being.

With the captain now gone, maybe the Far from the MCC now shared this view. ■

2014

Mike Reeves

TO the outsider, a cricket tour is a strange concept. The idea of 15-20 middle aged blokes spending three or four days together in twin beds at B&B's, surviving on a diet of cooked breakfasts, fast food and beer, playing matches against opposition of unknown strength and attitude, and doing goodness knows what (mainly revolving around drinking) in the long stretches of downtime between games, is not everyone's cup of tea. However Tour is a staple of many cricket teams and the Far from the MCC are no exception, with a catalogue of successful treks away from Oxfordshire meaning there is never a problem filling the teamsheets. The MAD have never suffered from the "will he, won't he" flaky responses described so wonderfully in Harry Thompson's semi -autobiographical Penguins Stopped Play. Essentially "I'm 99% certain I'll be able to tour," means "it's 1% likely that I will actually tour". No, when a MAD player commits, he commits.†

MAD Tours are generally a highlight of any season, providing a barrel of laughs and a copious array of cherished memories. That is apart from 2014, which was an exception, an outlier, a Tour so unremittingly awful that it nearly killed the whole idea of touring ever again. The two golden rules of touring were broken:

1. Never stay more than 20 minutes from a Pirate themed crazy golf course.
2. Never let Paddy Mellor do the organising.

A combination of bad planning and bad luck produced an excursion so inconceivably bad that its name can never be mentioned. Its only purpose was to serve as a reminder that however bad things are or could be, they cannot be a bad as the 2014 Tour. It will forever go by the name "f______ T______".

2014 started the same as 2010, 2011, 2012 and 2013, with the totally predictable

---

† *After many years of aborted commitment, Jon Newman-Robson would eventually clamber aboard the MAD Tour bus of 2017 to Minehead, although judging from his on-field success (or lack of), he maybe wished he hadn't.*

The power of symbolism

opening day hammering at the hands of Horspath CC. It is said that only an idiot does the same thing repeatedly whilst expecting a different outcome, however we are not idiots, we know the story that has been written and actually quite enjoy turning up to admire the advertising hoardings and sample the delicious tea before having our arses handed to us.

The new season brought a change in captaincy as Martin Westmoreland had become overstretched with the rigours of family life and a flourishing career, so handed the mantle over to former leader Ian Howarth. One of Ian's first actions as captain, other than losing the toss, was to give an opening spot to debutant Matthew John Reading. Matthew was certainly unusual and possibly unique to the team in that he had no prior connection to it. He had played a bit at school and was simply looking for a friendly cricket team in central Oxford (as advertised on our website), so turned up at nets, showing himself to be a competent batsman. So welcome to the team Matt, now open, against Horspath. The other thing to know about Mr Reading, or more specifically his time with the FFTMCC, is that he is possibly the unluckiest player in the history of the club. If there is a ball of the day, a miracle ball, or one that keeps low, Matthew will generally receive it within his very first over. Today was no exception and he was duly out for one, just avoiding the 'duck on debut' club.

Matthew also had a day to forget in the second match of the season away to the Nomads. Like their name indicates, this team are nomadic with no regular home pitch. They are mostly associated with Swindon and sometimes go under the oxymoronic name of the Nomads of Swindon, but on this occasion we ventured much further to Chippenham in deepest Wiltshire. Matthew was out first ball to one that both kept low and deviated off course. He then had to give Martin Westmoreland out LBW, before picking up the buffet award. Sometimes cricket really is a trying game.

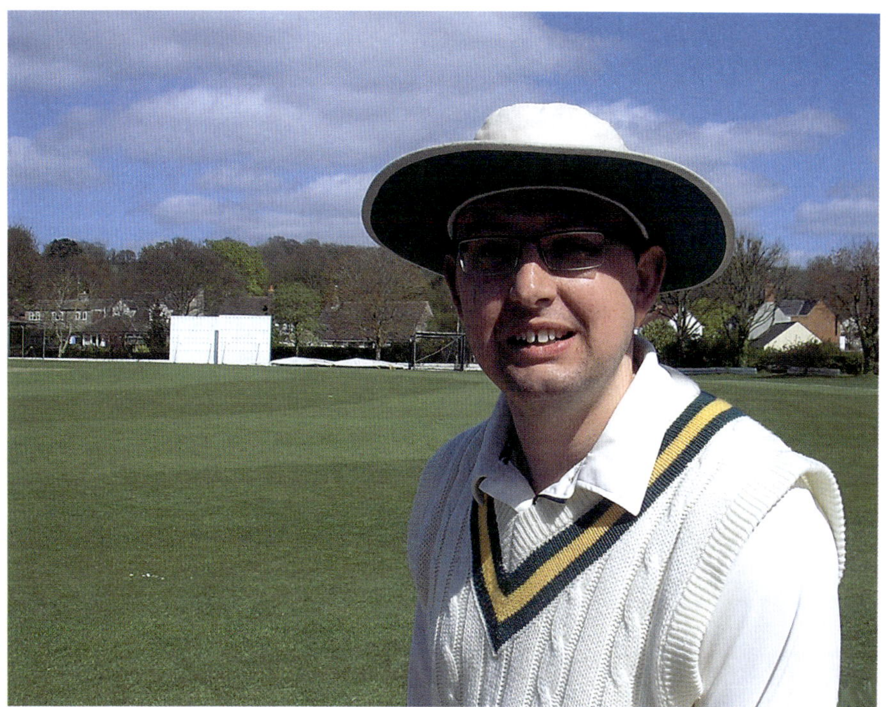

Do not stand behind Matt if war breaks out

The club were to lose three further matches prior to their first win of the season, the third of these being to regular opponents Oxford University Press (OUP) and their star batsman Chris Heron. Matches often hinged on whether 'Big Bird' (Heron, get it?) would fire and MAD confidence soared once he fell fourth ball to a screaming catch by Reeves in the gully. Unfortunately the match would be decided by a score of 40 from 'Judas' Jan Webster (his highest score for our side being 18).

The MAD's first win of 2014 did not come until game six of the season and a T20 away at Blewbury & Upton. I have always found this fixture a strange one given the home team's tinkering with the rules (sorry laws). Namely that every outfielder should bowl two overs and there are no LBW decisions. It's a tough one this, on the one hand I understand fully the level we're playing at and our severe deficiencies in the playing department. Also, that it's important that everyone feels involved and that they've had good value for their time and match fee. On the other hand though, what is the match, if not to marshal your resources to the best of your abilities? The match does throw up some welcome oddities though, wickets for Russ Turner for example. I'm happy to mark an asterisk against this game and move on.

In the final match in May, The MAD took on recent, but now favoured opponents Harwell CC. The international research facility at Harwell is reported home to a scaled down version of the Large Hadron Collider, or small large hadron collider if you like. No large hadrons appeared to be being colliding on this occasion, but the ground does have an air of mystery and 'government establishment' about it, as well as being one of the most massive we play on. On this occasion, The MAD did a great impression of eleven individuals who had forgotten how to bat and to listen to advice about batting. The match was also noteworthy for the debut of one Mark William Shelley. Mark was a former star player for the now defunct Marlborough House and coincidentally a work colleague of Ian Howarth. Mr Shelley has, as we say 'history' with another ex Marlbourite, Mike Reeves. The two do not see eye to eye on many things, principally Mark's inability to keep his big gob shut. The game renewed their relationship from six years previous as Mike dropped a catch off Mark's bowling, happy days.

June saw the Ebola virus taking hold in Southern Africa, whilst closer to home Carl Froch settled his differences with George Groves with one of the most blistering knockouts in UK fight history. On the Queen's College pitch against neighbours Isis CC, one MAD player also delivered a performance of devastating aggression and controlled hitting. Step forward James Pearson, who in front of a crowd of two (his parents) constructed a wonderful innings of 113 not out, the second highest in MAD history which also included a record six maximums in any one innings. This does however raise the sobering question of why James had whacked only nine sixes in his one hundred and eleven previous MAD knocks. This outstanding batting would duly earn James the Adie Fisher Performance of the Season award, in a match curiously notable for no MAD fathers in the team, or so we thought, until Mr Turner owned up to a previously polygamist lifestyle. Finally there was a supposed five MAD players taking a shower at the very same time, but more on showering later….

As already documented, cricket grounds range from the wonderful (Queen's College) to the bloody awful (Holton during Ramadan), but in 2014 the team were introduced to another gem. Cumnor cricket ground is located just up the hill to the west of Oxford, but surprisingly most of the team were not aware of its existence until a T20 against the Bodleian. Games against the librarians are eagerly anticipated because: (a) they're a jolly good bunch and (b) we usually win. Moving the game to a Friday evening at a wonderful location, with its pavilion and bar perched on a small rise overlooking the pitch has set this fixture as one the most enjoyable of any season.

Isis only had to wait nine days for their revenge against James Pearson et al, rolling over The MAD at Brasenose on a warm and pleasant summer evening T20. Jonah, aka Matthew Reading, got his second Golden of the year, to one that was almost certainly the ball of the day.

As surely as night follows day and Horspath deliver a hammering, so The MAD are expected to take an annual dicking from the Lemmings. That this game happened at all is testament to the resourcefulness and resolve of The MAD organising committee as the scheduled Brasenose pitch was announced "unavailable" only an hour or so before the game. That we would be letting down one of our longest standing rivals was one thing, but the realisation that Steve Dobner was already on route from Essex was quite another and therefore desperate phone calls were made to anyone in Oxfordshire with access to a strip of turf of more than 22 yards in length. Amazingly Jordan Hill was procured with the minimum of notice and the teams headed to North Oxford. Despite the fact that on this day The Lemmings were not fielding any former members of the England woman's cricket team, they still won, however the margin of 23 runs represents the closest we have ever, or may ever come to rolling them over.

It is at this point we return to a subject signposted earlier, showering. One would expect that after five hours of running around on a warm afternoon that a shower would be necessary to cleanse the body and soul. It is therefore a constant surprise that such a low number of the team choose to take this option. Like cricket grounds, the showers also vary markedly and can be ranked. At the bottom of the list are places like Cholsey and in particular Aston Tirrold, where the word shower is used optimistically. These facilities deliver more of a fine mist such as one would experience in the Amazon rain forest and the only option is to set all sprinklers going and then wander aimlessly around until one is suitably damp. There's also Enstone, where players rush to secure a spot at the opposite end of the changing room as the "cubicle" in "shower cubicle" is more notional than constructional, leaving kit bags drenched. Most grounds, such as Brasenose (good water pressure and direction, although shower trays about the size of a tea tray†), Oriel (good sized individual cubicles, but a strange green algae at about knee height) and Jesus College (great, except the sign to clean boots outside seems never to have been read) provide perfectly reasonable ablution facilities. Top of the list are the likes of Harwell and Magdalen College, where one is tempted to not only shower, but to bring along any clothes, kids, dogs and gardening implements that also require a clean. Like many aspects of The MAD, showering has its darker side and the origins of the standard fine "showering with Nick" remain a mystery.

Towards the end of June the team went on a rare, but very welcome winning streak of four matches. Mike Reeves shone with both bat and ball against Enstone scoring an unbeaten 29* and taking 5-12, whilst Dave Shorten's dog Midge, club mascot, tried to reduce the local population of infant Muntjac deer by the tune of one. The MAD's good form was in stark contrast to England's abysmal performance at the World Cup in Brazil.

Over the years there remained a handful of teams this club had never savoured victory against. Horspath and the Lemmings were always considered a class above, but one team who consistently held the upper hand, was due in no small part to our side simply throwing it all away. We turn of course to Milton (away) and the eight long years since 2006 when The MAD witnessed its biggest collapse in history, going from 99-1 to 108

† *this was prior to the 2017 refurbishment, after which there is little to complain about*

Just me hanging out with Duck

all out after a drinks break. Those eight years had been potted with highs, lows, cobs, more cobs, a fifty from Andrew Darley, a carrying of the bat by Howarth and a visit to the hospital by Jake (same match), but still no victory. On paper this never seemed an enticing fixture. For one thing it was miles away from Oxford and as has been discussed many times before, almost a mini tour in itself, albeit one distasteful to the mouth. So a typical day would be, drive nearly an hour to Marco Pier White's gaff (The Black Boy pub) for a pre-match drink with some Morris dancers, suffer an afternoon of self-inflicted disappointment, suffer the indignity of no shower and pissing behind a wooden shed which doubled as a pavilion, then return to Marco's to rue the experience and fine everyone into pecuniary oblivion. Despite all of this, Milton (away) still remained one of the most eagerly anticipated fixtures with an overflow of players wanting to finally get the monkey off our back and utter the immortal words, "I was there." I remember little of the game itself, but the scorecard shows the standout performance being from Dave Shorten with figures of 7.4-5-14-4. Afterwards I remember there was a feeling of almost anti-climax. It would have been fitting after all that time if the match had been won in a last ball thriller or an inspirational moment from a deserving individual, but in reality it was just a workmanlike performance with contributions all round. In the years that followed, the incentive was gone and the fixture was dropped.

During the latter part of July there were further losses to Astons CC and Ralph Smith and also to Garsington in a T20, this despite a record breaking unbroken partnership of 122* from Ian Howarth and Russ Turner. The rest of July saw fine weather and a string of pleasant if unremarkable matches with a win against Isis here and a loss to Appleton there. All that changed in August with a standout performance which lifted Dave Shorten clear of the pack and propelled him towards an almost clean sweep of the trophies at the AGM. A century is always a truly remarkable thing and as of 2017, only ten have ever been scored for the club in well over 400 matches, but even by those rarefied standards, this particular one was special. The fact that he'd never even passed fifty previously and the fact that it came off just 86 balls and achieved with a huge six are all amazing, but seeing that the rest of the team scored a paltry 40 runs between them makes this one of the greatest innings of this or any other season. Gary Timms reported that his decision to award the Adie Fisher Performance of the Season award was an especially difficult one and by a hair's breadth it couldn't be given to Dave, because through no fault of his (and despite the fact he also got a run out), it was in a losing cause as Islip romped home with almost ten overs to spare.

And so to Tour and things started to go badly awry even before we'd set off. This year's tour organiser, Patrick Mellor had secured for us the Lord Hill Hotel which is, to quote its website "ideally situated on the outskirts of Shrewsbury" and just across the road from our Friday evening opponents Wroxeter Grove CC. Club Treasurer and general organiser Mike Reeves rang the hotel a few days before just to confirm the numbers and sort out any final details.

"Ring ring, ring ring."

LHH: "Hello, Lord Hill Hotel, outskirts of Shrewsbury, how can I help you?"
MR: "Oh hi, Mike Reeves here, treasurer and current player of the year from the FFTMCC, just ringing to check that everything is in place for the visit of myself and my thirteen team mates for what is sure to be four days of heavy drinking and putting hundreds of pounds behind your bar."

Shorten slogging his way into folklore

LHH: "Ah yes, about that. We've been trying to contact a P Mellor from your organisation, but he's changed his email address and phone number."
MR: "Okay."
LHH: "Yes, in the absence of you re-confirming your confirmation, we've decided to give all your rooms away to those more interested in looking at flowers than playing cricket."
MR: "Flowers?"
LHH: "Yes, it's the annual flower festival here in Shrewsbury (and on its outskirts). Busiest weekend of the year in fact. Flower viewers come from miles around to you know, look at some flowers."
MR: "So my chances of finding another room in the Shrewsbury area?"
"Bbbrrrrrrrrrrrrrrr."
MR: "Hello…?"

So the hunt started for alternative accommodation. As the hours and days passed by the search area was widened and the standards dropped. Eventually after a multitude of emails, phone calls and split decisions, the Holiday Inn, in (whisper it) Telford was chosen, on the basis that it could accommodate all 14 of us and was marginally nearer to Shrewsbury than Oxford was.

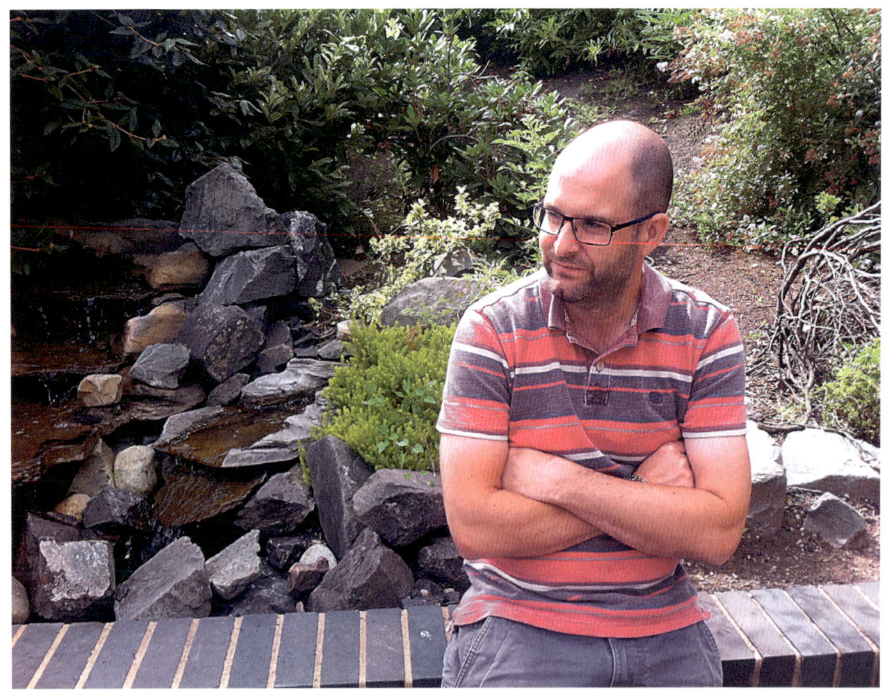

Steve Dobner contemplates the cancelled game

It was still with a sense of optimism that the team travelled up the M40 on the Thursday morning and congregated in the garden of the Holiday Inn in anticipation of an evening's T20 match up. Only when the team was almost fully assembled was it announced that the opposition currently only had four players and even counting three potential Judas's from our side, this was simply not viable. James Pearson was phoned to say don't even bother making the trip. He was thus luckily spared the shambles to come.

Friday started with the search for something to do in the hours before another evening T20. Bizarrely, in Telford this included two crazy golf courses and literally nothing else. Crazy golf Number One was 'Wonderland' which included a piped theme tune played all over the course, which is permanently ingrained in the brain to anyone who listens to it. The 18 holes were made entirely of concrete which was like putting on a sheet of ice. Crazy golf course Number Two could not have been more different, a thoroughly professional but somehow soulless, astroturf experience. As morning turned into opening time, it was right to start looking for drinking establishments in Telford. These were found to consist exclusively of a Chinese restaurant and the tenpin bowling arena. It was at about this time, after several jugs of warm Fosters in the 'Tenpin' that Telford was re-christened fucking Telford, ever to be written as f______ T______.

With no game scheduled for the Saturday, Martin Westmoreland spent a good part of Friday on the phone, trying to procure tickets for the 4th Test at Old Trafford against India.

"Ring ring, ring ring."

LCCC: "Hello, Lancashire County Cricket Club."
MW: "Oh, hi there. Martin Westmoreland here, FFTMCC tour social secretary and 2010 Player of the Season. Myself and twelve of my cricket playing associates would like to purchase tickets for tomorrow's play in the 4th Test against India."
LCCC: "Certainly Sir, but tickets can only be purchased by members of Lancashire County Cricket Club."
MW: "Oh dear, that's a pity."
LCCC: "Never mind, I can take you through the extremely lengthy application process on the phone now if you like, whilst your colleagues wait in nervous anticipation of being able to get out of f______ T______ tomorrow."
MW: "That sounds a reasonable idea."
[Some considerable time later….] LCCC: "Well Sir, that seems to be the forms filled out in triplicate, may I ask why you want to join LCCC?"
MW: "I want to buy tickets for the Test tomorrow, remember?"
LCCC: "Certainly Sir, we have one left, do you want it?"
"Bbbrrrrrrrrrrrrrr."

Friday evening saw what was to be the one and only tour game in not so nearby

On account of this cricket tour being unforgettably forgettable – game of golf anyone?

Shrewsbury. After a lengthy coach journey to the ground, where the team admired where they could have stayed, it was decided, on the advice of pub guru Matt Bullock to walk the several further miles in to town in search of a CAMRA recommended pub. Matt is rarely wrong, but on this occasion, he directed his teammates past several suitable watering holes, to the CAMRA recommended one, which was… shut. Still, we did get to look at some flowers.

The Friday game itself was enjoyable enough with some of their team smacking enormous sixes over the nearby council offices, and Dobner and Reeves hitting smaller ones just over the boundary rope. The game was notable for two of the most incompetent pieces of fielding ever witnessed from Messieurs Carter and Rundle, Geoff somehow incapable of stopping a stationary ball before booting it for four, and 'Psycho' steadying himself perfectly under a steepler only to see it land ten metres to his left. An abortive run-chase would then ensue with over 8,000 runs in the form and Howarth and Westmoreland simply watching from the boundary. After the game the teams retreated into the Wroxeter clubhouse where we were all told to keep quiet because the bingo was in progress. Despite this, Tour virgin Gary Timms, provided a quiz with questions revolving around "who am I?" It became an instant classic and is sure to be repeated in subsequent years. Considering what a thoroughly anti-climactic and disastrous weekend it was as a whole, this was literally the highlight.

On the Saturday, instead of watching the professionals play in Manchester the team travelled to watch two local, but far superior (to us) teams play. They even did proper warming up and everything. It was during this afternoon that we learnt that the remnants of hurricane Bertha was on its way and would bring high winds and torrential rain to parts of Shropshire. At this point all remaining hope was extinguished and the team decided to cut their losses and head back to Oxfordshire a day early. The name f_____ T______ had passed into MAD history books, only to be spoken of in hushed tones from that day forward. The team were so demoralised and shell-shocked that they ended the season with four further defeats, including Howarth terminating his role as transitional Captain several games early. That fateful decision came after opting to bowl first on an "extremely helpful pitch" in Appleton and watching aghast as the home side piled up 241-3. Sitting out the tea interval to consider his options, he angrily opted to front the reply, attempting to hit the first ball of the innings for six and being castled for a golden duck. His day was made complete on return to the pavilion, with Mark Rundle offering sarcastic words of encouragement by way of "well batted, skip…."

The AGM that year belonged to one man and one man only. Dave Shorten (270 runs at 19.29 and 21 wickets at 18.00) would pick up Player of the Season, Most Improved Player, Champagne Moment and even bagged the Fantasy Cricket winnings (FFS). He was only denied the Performance of the Season due to that outstanding 113* from James Pearson and the fact that he would have needed an extra carrier bag to get his haul home. ■

2014 was all about Mr Shorten

2015

Ian Howarth

UNDER the youthful supervision of Gary Timms, 2015 would mark a return to winning ways, at least since the era of beating shitty pub teams. Of course pub teams don't really exist anymore, likewise most of the shitty pubs themselves. Even if they do, we don't play them anymore, save for the Bell Inn which is in fact Aldworth CC, and isn't a shitty pub. We're not even a pub team ourselves these days. We haven't been affiliated with a drinking establishment since briefly being the Far from the Royal Oak (on Woodstock Road) a decade ago, but we never renamed or rebranded and the landlady buggered off before we had *that* discussion. So who are we then? Opinions vary, we are likened to "a pub team full of ringers" when we win, and dismissed as "a pub team full of losers" when we lose. Our own consensus is that we're just a nomadic collection of guys who like a drink and a laugh, enjoy a win now and again, and are delighting in growing old together under a fictional name against non-fictional opposition. But of course, if a landlord or landlady reads this and sees fit to throw us a pile of cash (or chips and sausages), we'll happily sell our soul (and name) to the highest bidder.

This aforementioned resurgence in form wasn't all about Mr Timms however, there was another guy helping to breathe life back into the team. Nobody else within the club can match the zestful, gladdening and eccentric zeal of Dave Shorten, who after a decade of bit parts under the stupefying dictatorships of Howarth and Westmoreland, decided T20 cricket *was* for him and he wanted to tailor it to his own gratifying likings. Thus it was that The MAD were catapulted into a world without fear or recrimination, one where anything could be achieved and the sky was the limit.

For a year of such unparalleled success, it didn't exactly start auspiciously with a contentious defeat away at Cholsey Meadows. In the shadow of the adjoining Fair Mile lunatic asylum, antipodean Chris Hansen (88*) led his team to 1 wicket win after surviving a plumb LBW shout with the scores tied. Despite repeated appeals from bowler Ian Howarth, the home umpire was having none of it, and the genial Aussie would later admit over a beer to it being "pretty bloody close". It was Chris, it was pretty bloody *out*. There was also a final trip to play in Islip, a historical Oxfordshire village boasting a turd of a pitch at odds with its quaint and enchanting surrounds. Chasing not a great deal, The MAD were indebted to Gary Timms' high score of 9 in achieving even less than not a great deal, before deciding never again.

May 19 is a day that will probably linger in Dave Shorten's memory, but for all the wrong reasons. In only his second game in charge, inclement weather in Blewbury caused an acrimonious split in The MAD camp. Having pissed it down a quarter of an hour earlier and with thundery clouds looming ominously on the horizon, arriving players divided into three pools: of naysaying depressives, the confused of thought and rose-tinted optimists. Political to-and-froing then ensued, eventually degenerating into a heated debate, finger pointing and Dave's tools eventually being thrown out of his work's van, with certain team members being told to go forth and multiply. With only seven MAD upbeats willing to start the match, despite a positive Blewbury vote, the doom-mongers held sway and the match was called off. The team then drove home in silence and bright sunshine. Much has been written about cricket and the weather. The two are interminably intertwined, and those who remember 'Woodstock 2013' will never *ever* forget, less start a game of cricket in the bleeding rain. Call us miserable bastards, Dave, we really don't care, but Dave may we all welcome you to the joys of Captaincy and all it entails.

The weather map says yes, but you f_____ are saying no

The springboard for an otherwise joyous year began a few days earlier, with a 44 run victory over the OUP whilst playing "away" at our "home" ground of Brasenose. Reliant on Matt Bullock's season high 32 to rescue a pitiful innings, The MAD defended in style thanks to the *Hoskins & Rundle* show, or should that read the other way around? We're well-versed in the legendary piemanship of 'Dobber' Hoskins, the famed village sorcerer of flan, but maybe less attuned to the lamentable, wholly unremarkable, shuffling military medium dross of Mark Rundle. Having studied the IT industry's laziest worker first hand and faced this doleful psychopathic menace in the nets, I simply can't comprehend how he does it (take wickets). Trundling in like he's shit his leg from a late night kebab, he grimaces whilst wricking his shoulder, throwing you down some innocuous beef and relish. It begs to be hit, just implores you to shimmy out your crease and belt the ball into the middle of Istanbul. But that's just the problem, as any batting success is immediately decoded in that well-hidden brain of his as he sneakily pulls his length back just-ever-so slightly. As was the case here in taking 4 -19 to rip out OUP's top order, before a tasteful quip in my direction to "stick that in your pipe Howarth and f______ smoke it!"

Another curiosity of non-league cricket is that of dual citizenship. Or in plain English, a guy who can't make his mind up where his allegiances are. With no stipulation to *sign on* for a friendly team, this individual can represent whomever he sees fit on any given day, just as long as he sticks his hand in his wallet at the bar before and afterwards and pays his subs. A case example would be Johannes van den Grootschnyke Webster, player #123 when available for The MAD, and player #JudasTurncoatBastard when available for the OUP. Of studious mien and with a name of Sri Lankan proportions in terms of length, "our Janny" is identifiable as the tall and erratic bespectacled chappy, rouge of the face as though he's escaped from a chemistry lab. Professor Webster didn't represent anyone on this day, preferring instead to double up as a neutral umpire in his science overalls and a journalist by way of a match report.

After Shorten's un-Shortenlike 37* off 86 balls to claim a win away at Harwell International, there followed some curious melodrama in the climax of a T20 win at Hanney. With batsman J Hilliam switching stance from RHB to LHB and back again during the final two deliveries, bowler Howarth simply speared the ball down leg. Two dot balls were the verdict of the umpire and The MAD triumphed by a mere 7 runs. With an incendiary batsman and ongoing animation within the home team changing room, an online ticket† was raised concerning the laws of the game.

With the season in danger of becoming successful, including wins one and two of four against neighbours Isis CC, the team were then brought back to reality, firstly by the caveman club of Gary Dogget (60) on that shitty school pitch, and then by the infinitely less brutal, nay consummate skills of the ex-University fellows the Lemmings. A thirteenth consecutive defeat to the latter stuck in the craw somewhat, especially after

---

† Law 25.1(a) – Judging a Wide... the umpire shall adjudge it a Wide if... the ball passes wide of the striker where he is and which also would have passed wide of him standing in a normal guard position.

Law 25.2(a) – Delivery not a Wide... the umpire shall not adjudge a delivery as being a Wide if the striker, by moving, either
(i) causes the ball to pass wide of him... or
(ii) brings the ball sufficiently within his reach to be able to hit it by means of a normal cricket stroke.

Suffice to say, that by changing stance, the batsman (Mr Hilliam) gave up the normal "leg-side" Wide adjudication. Henceforth, the Hanney umpire was vindicated, if not invited back to the home team pub afterwards.

Hadfield (left) discussing the percentage of inbreeding in Hanney with Mr Ainsworth

restricting the intellectual rodents to just 148-7. The MAD then limped to a 41 run defeat despite having on paper what was regarded as a stellar line-up†, though whether this was inked on the toilet variety is open to discussion.

As the migrant crisis in the Mediterranean gripped the world, the second half of June and into July was almost total MAD domination, with T20 Smith (30* and 2-17)

† *One of the real headaches of Sunday captaincy is giving everyone a fair crack of the whip whilst also remaining competitive. Indeed in recent years, Messrs Timms and Shorten have used advanced algorithmic spreadsheets to ensure all sub-paying servants are given their time at the table. Only a few fixtures remain outside of these parameters (such as the Lemmings and Cup games etc), where theirs is carte blanche in picking their best and most in-form eleven. Not that it is openly discussed, as failing to make 'that' team could then lead to days of defamatory emails ping-ponging around as players vent their spleen.*

Once upon a time, Skipper Howarth sent out a team sheet containing in his own words "the strongest eleven to meet the requirements". Days later, legendary landlord and ultimate poker host, James Hoskins, informed Ian that tenant and co-cricketer Andrew Cavanagh had discussed at length about wrapping a bat around his head. Lesson learnt.

excelling by the sewage plant in Appleton and Turner (51) and everyone else filling their boots at Jordan Hill against Enstone. Throughout these heady times, the genial giant of Chris Roberts was having the season of his life. A fresh and confident swagger had replaced the stuttering imperfections of yore, and Bob was now galloping in, swinging the ball in from height and taking wickets a bundle. In harmony with his teammate, believing any ball of any length could be summarily twatted, Mr Shorten had also gone into overdrive, his bludgeoning of 42* off 23 balls at Queens College a part of the dizzying 161-9 thumped against Isis in the third encounter (second T20).

Every season has a standout performance, a shortlisted feat now recognised by those still sober enough to vote at the end of season AGM. Adrian Fisher (after whom the trophy is posthumously named) would no doubt have been proud of two of the contesting efforts, coming as they did just three weeks apart, and from the same treasured bat. Infinitely unreliable and mercurially breathtaking when he gets it right, David Emerson stuck two fingers up to fellow Centricite Ralph Smith as he blazed 59* off just 42 balls to help chase down the 183-8 of Astons CC. Soaked in alcohol, it was a fantastically fearless display of hitting through the V, only usurped by his opening salvo against Islip, a match where Dave plundered 47 off 26 balls including 22 off an over from opening bowler Farooq. He was out with the score on 56-1, a dismal collapse foreshadowing an eventual MAD victory with Shorten's runs at the death.

Then, all of a sudden, it was time to put the tumultuous misery of f______ T______ to bed, and undertake that most arduous yet rapturous weekends in The MAD sporting calendar, Tour. Four days and three *long* evenings in Hythe & Dibden, Hampshire, to balance being utterly wankered with creditable shows on the pitch. D-Day can be considered Thursday, rendezvousing at said destination† in shared cars and work vans,

Emerson in fine fettle at Harwell International

† *The destination and hotelier for this particular stay was the rather lively Fountain Court Hotel. Lovingly lampooned as 'Balti Towers' the following year, with its Indian owners and somewhat chaotic undertaking reminding everyone of the John Cleese classic.*

Reeves about to give the keeper a good beat down

delighting in Stuart Broad's 8-15 in the fourth Ashes Test, bellowing at each arriving face and getting down to the serious business of buying rounds. Having all assembled, players are then drawn out of a hat to see who can get really shitfaced, and those that have to retain a modicum of awareness for the game(s) ahead. Skippers are also appointed for each game from a handful of enthusiasts, one of whom will wish he never volunteered as long as he lives.

With Reeves' 39* unable to wrest victory in an enjoyable T20 romp at Sarisbury, attention turned to the harbour town itself on the Friday, and later to Roberts and Howarth who had spent the entire day down the pub. A great match report likened their nomenclature to the characters "in John Steinbeck's masterpiece of American literature 'Of Mice and Men', [one] a gentle giant, whereas the other was much smaller and also more world weary. However they differed in several key aspects, in that Lennie and George were sober, whilst the heroes of our tale were several sheets to the wind. Also for Steinbeck, George was the brains of the outfit, whereas with this pair it was difficult to tell where the intelligence lay." Already regretting his role, Captain Pearson was thankful to Lennie's fifteenth† pint removing him from any team sheet, however he was less lucky with a demonstratively hammered Howarth. Somehow James engineered a tie with the teams on 175 after 25 overs, and somehow he kept George free from a cricketing injury.

George (45) and Lennie (14*) were immeasurably less plastered the following day at the Trojans CC and helped by Timms' (29) revelatory role with the bat, T. P. W. Smith rode a MAD horse to victory for the first time in almost 6 years. Ironically, the last tour victory was *also* secured under his stewardship, black and white film stock recording the event at Legbourne in Lincoln.

† *Pure speculation, though this may and probably was an underestimate*

With all to play for on the Sunday, the tourists' final match was staged in the palatial surrounds of Pylewell Park, a sumptuously dreamy New Forest estate boasting a cricket team with a 150 year history and a pavilion with a thatched roof. A wonderful tour was cemented by victory on a glorious English summer's day, with James Pearson's 52* (off 37 balls) or Steve Dobner's diamond duck being the highlight depending on your predilection. All four of the hosting clubs deserve the utmost praise, respecting the ethos of Tour and picking teams to suit. They would we welcome to Oxfordshire should they ever decide.

It is often mooted that the season feels *over* on completion of Tour, some would say the Far from the MCC felt over after f______ T______. Lethargic and casual in defeat at Wytham, this undulating little ground off the A34 with a squeezed artificial strip somehow seemed to epitomise the comedown. Even Dobner's two ball duck barely merited a giggle, after Glastonbury what highlights are there left in the festival year? Certainly nothing at Jordan Hill, where in an abhorrent display versus OUP, Reeves (46) was the only MAD batsman to get double figures. However, #JudasTurncoatBastard did impress with an unbeaten 7, albeit for the other team.

Less fatigued and battle scarred than his predecessors, Captain Timms somehow found a resolve to complete the season. After securing the double in the rain and mud of

The gorgeous ground of Pylewell CC.

Aston Tirrold, a Richard Hadfield (45 off 92 balls) inspired victory over Isis at a vapid Stanton St. John represented the most successful MAD season *ever*, at least in terms of games won. Despite no new faces, The MAD notched up a staggering twenty victories (none under Vice R. P. Turner), two ties (none under Vice R. P. Turner), and eleven defeats (three under Vice R. P. Turner), for a final win ratio of 60.61%. It was a percentage only bettered in 2007 (64.71%) when the club weren't involved in any T20s, Howarth could bat and Antony Mann was a figurehead amongst bowling riches. A keen statistician immediately cross-references the opposition of these seasons in looking for a Zimbabwe-factor†, but there was none forthcoming, other than the two wins apiece over the Bodleian.

Spare a thought for the above referenced R. P. Turner, because if there was *one* man the team would dearly have loved to come up trumps for, it was him. At this point in his fledgling MAD career, Russ' Captaincy CV†† read won 0, drawn 0, lost 9, having never *once* shirked filling the breach or putting his belly above the parapet. A popular, generous and endlessly enigmatic member of the club, his day would come.

But what were the reasons for this transformation from habitual losers to magnificent winners? Why was 2015 such a great year to be around the club, with The MAD for once avoiding the time honoured cliché of turning triumph into disaster? The change in leadership was an obvious factor, but to gaze upon the averages was revealing, with no fewer than *eight* players scoring over 250 runs and many solid contributions elsewhere. There was seemingly no reliance on one or two individuals anymore, with wickets also being shared about. At the ever popular end of season piss-up* / AGM* / Kangaroo Court* (*delete as appropriate), a boisterous contingent universally agreed Dave Shorten (384 runs at 21.33, 22 wickets at 15.55) retain his *Player of the Season* award ahead of the *Most Improved* victor Chris Roberts (32 wickets at 19.06). But there were many other candidates, the evergreen Reeves shone again with 349 runs at 21.81 to complement 28 wickets at 16.61, James Pearson stroked 355 runs at 29.58 and also took 11 wickets (at 19.55), a topsy-turvy Howarth hit 421 runs at 23.39, with the dependable Turner weighing in with 358 runs at 19.89. And of course not forgetting The MAD's greatest bowler this millennium, James Hoskins, out-flighted and out-darted another 24 silly buggers at 16.71. Dave Emerson (297 runs at 24.75) would pick up a deserved *Performance of the Season* for his opening blitz against Islip.

With the curtain now descending and the AGM degenerating into an inebriated Sambuca drinking contest, all that was left was for Dave Shorten's shitfaced ego to

† *The Zimbabwe-factor is a rather unkind reference to the crappiest team in international cricket, whose vested interest seems solely to boost the win column of the opposition and distort their respective averages (and or HS or BB). Before their fortunes swung in recent years, it was formerly known as the Bangladesh-factor, and in village parlance it continues to be known as the Bodleian-factor.*

†† *Russ has unfortunately never skippered a game against the Bodleian.*

Jon Newman (right) giving Shorten the stare down

decide that having conquered the world of cricket, he would now turn his not inconsiderable talents to arm wrestling. An ill-fated decision, any early success would be offset by his shoulder and bicep failing to withstand the pumped-up thirty two wickets and nearly-man status of Tall Bob. ■

2016

Mike Reeves

2016 was the year that western democracy lost its collective marbles. It was as if everyone suddenly adopted the attitude of a relapsing alcoholic, as in "this is almost certainly a bad idea but to hell with it, let's try it anyway." Examples being, "screw it, let's alienate our closest allies and trading partners, I'm sure it'll be fine." Or "I'm sure an egomaniac billionaire has our best interests at heart, let's put him in charge." In a world of uncertainty people were looking for some consistency, a small haven where the same petty rivalries would go unresolved year after year. Welcome, once again, to another season at the FFTMCC.

Jan Webster sprinted out of the blocks to start the 2016 season. His first act was to smack his head off the lintel above the door of the Red Lion in Cholsey before even a coin had been tossed. He then gave an expansive "leave" to a ball on off stump whilst still on nought and then, to put the tin hat on his day, he left his borrowed bat in the changing room. Someone who was genuinely off to a fast start was Lee Ainsworth, who recorded a 45 not out and a 50 in the first two games of the season, picking up consecutive Man of the Match awards and guiding the team to wins away at Cholsey and Enstone. This despite his team mates dropping a collective twelve catches in those first two outings. Enstone was its typical Siberian self in what was one of the coldest games we'd played since the last time we visited a windswept hilltop north of Oxford in late April. Enstone's alternative name of Estonia was now permanently frozen into the collective consciousness.

May Day saw the traditional closing of Magdalen bridge (pronounced Maudlin by everyone except Paddy) to stop students compacting their spinal cords, whilst The MAD visited Wytham CC. A particularly strange game, on paper Wytham ticks all the boxes. It boasts a decent, secluded ground close to Oxford, a very good tea and a nice cosy pub for afterwards and yet somehow, we never really clicked with the team. Some of our other rivals have reported a similar feeling and so we ditched them, along with their two-inch wide artificial wicket for the following season. For the record, in a match where 45 runs were accumulated through wides, The MAD won out with James Hoskins picking up yet another four-for.

Ainsworth batting the wrong way round

One of the many joys of living in Oxford is the number of cricket grounds close to the city centre. Viewing a photo of Oxford from the air shows at least twenty inside the ring road. It's unfortunate that many of them are for the exclusive use of the University Colleges, although some of the more socially and financially minded are coming to realise that renting them out provides a useful income stream. The MAD have played at most of them over the years, but for the first T20 of the season against Wolvercote, the team went in search of a new venue somewhere off the Woodstock Road. Having searched most of North Oxford, trespassing through fields and tennis courts, the ground was eventually located, and the team promptly bowled out for 88. This first loss of the season was followed up by a dispiriting loss to the OUP, this despite the impressive Ainsworth scoring over 50% of a MAD total with 83. The match was dispiriting for several reasons: (a) we were truly awful (b) Lee really should have bagged a ton and (c) it was played at the soulless environs of Horspath recreation ground, nuff said.

Much has already been written about trying to balance the requirements of winning and having a good game. No-one enjoys being on the receiving end of a one-sided match, but also delivering a thrashing against an under-strength opposition usually feels hollow and pointless. This is just part of the many reasons why The MAD have no interest in playing league games. However, in 2016 we were invited to enter our first proper cup competition, the Friendly Cup. I say proper cup competition because The MAD had actually competed for silverware before. Who can forget the 6-aside debacle of 2011, or the super over debacle of 2012? The Friendly Cup was definitely a step up from these one day competitions, this time it would be eight sides battling it out over three rounds on a series of Sundays.

The Ying and Yang of "friendly" and "cup" were put to the test in the first round against Aldworth, with the opposition team being decimated by a wedding occurring on the same day as the game. Aldworth slumped to 13-5 and with no-one over ten years of age padded up it looked like the game would be over in short order. There were murmurings of "make a game of it" from the opposition, but what were we to do? How demoralising would it have felt all round if they'd gone on to win? Captain Timms did his best to inject some sort of life into proceedings by turning to non-bowler Mr Turner, but with even him (no offence Russ) taking two wickets, what exactly is a captain to do? Like I said, all a little hollow and a little pointless, but The MAD did march on the semi-finals, whilst both Moo and Timms moved on to 100 career wickets and Howarth was bowled by a child for a second ball duck.

Talking of miss-matches and (referencing the start of this chapter) petty rivalries perpetuating year after year, what is it with J Higgs of St Clements Strollers? Will he ever get bored of flogging us to all parts of Magdalen (it's pronounced Maudlin Paddy) college ground? We don't think so. His 52 not out this year was utterly predictable, but what is a man to do?

As we reach the later stages of this tome, we find that we are frequently returning to themes already covered and in that regard we must speak again of what a thoroughly nice bloke Russ Turner is. His willingness to pitch in is particularly noticeable with regards to captaincy. Russ is the vice captain's vice captain and therefore by definition when he is leading the team, we have been sorely depleted. It is therefore no reflection on Russ himself that at the start of 2016 his captaincy record read played nine, won

Turner proving that any old shit can take wickets

zero, drawn zero, tied zero, zero abandoned. Yes, that's nine solid, undeniable, straight forward stuffings. Would he reach double figures during the visit to Harwell in late May? Not on your nelly, well stuck at it dude.

At times, cricket seems like a sport almost designed to ensure the physical and mental breakdown of those who choose to participate in it. At our level it's generally played by middle aged men who have sedentary jobs and undertake little in the way of sporting activity other than one or two games a week. The game itself largely consists of standing around for long periods, interspersed with short, intense bursts of energy. The action of bowling exposes shoulders, knees, backs, ankles and hips to entirely unnatural movements. It's really a wonder that any of us are standing at all. For those that are, the weekly diet of disappointment and crushing underachievement is almost indigestible.

In 2016 it was the left knee of Mike Reeves that saw him side-lined for several matches. Historically there was of course Howarth and his hernia, Westmoreland and his dodgy hamstrings, Dobner and his excruciating shin splints, then Emerson and his on-going shoulder problem which has of course transmogrified into an occasional Achilles problem segueing into a quad problem. However, chief amongst the sick notes are Mark Rundle and Richard Hadfield. Mark's body is a walking (shuffling) advertisement for glorious triumph of desire over a complete absence of athleticism. Every time he runs (shuffles) in to bowl the team wait with baited breadth to see if he'll finally collapse into that sorry heap of broken parts we all know constitute his body. Richard Hadfield is an entirely different animal. He closely resembles a Formula One racing car, firing on all cylinders before exploding in a cinematic tour de force of overacting before being rushed off to the John Radcliffe. Lest we forget those who can't handle a hangover, James Pearson's tally of non-appearances due to intoxication is shameful. The fact he has cried off whilst looking after the scorebook makes it even worse.

There is then the mental disintegration, which has been documented by David Frith and others. It would be fair to say that everyone has their cricketing demons, but perhaps chief amongst them are Jan Webster and (again) Martin Westmoreland. Both find enterprising, novel, unlucky and infuriating ways to get themselves out despite no lack of talent. Jan also frequently loses his head and the wicket of his teammate in runout fiascos. The MAD even find ways to injure themselves and their teammates when not playing cricket. Back in the mists to time there is the infamous 'dancing injury' of James Hoskins and also the 'kettle injury' sustained by Jake Hotson.

In 2016 The MAD committee decided that there simply weren't enough awards presented at the AGM. To the list of Player of the Season, Most Improved Player, Performance of the Year, Champagne Moment, Clubman of the year and Fantasy Team winner† was to be added the MAD Moment of the Year and The MAD Booker prize.

---

† *I'm always mystified why we provide a trophy to the fantasy league winner, seeing that they already pocket around £120 for winning it. Maybe it's because they're expected to immediately cough it up for Sambucas all round.*

More on The MAD Moment later, but The MAD Booker prize, which of course takes its name from the UK's premier literary fiction award, the Man Booker prize, was intended to reward the works of "scripted reality" i.e. the website match reports. It was intended to encourage those members of the team who rarely, if ever, volunteer to pen a match report to throw their literary hat in to the ring. However, in reality it simply and immediately engendered an intense rivalry between Reeves and Howarth into who could, in the eyes of their teammates, write the best report. Sod who's better at playing cricket, it was now all about who's better at writing about cricket. On the 3rd June, The MAD played the Bodleian. Howarth wasn't playing, but instead got pissed and penned the bigoted, post-Brexit report "Me and Geoff", which duly went on to scoop the inaugural MAD Booker prize and gave Reeves one more reason to bitch at the AGM.

During one of the long sunlit days of June, The MAD inflicted one of their four unanswered victories over Isis during a T20 at Jesus College. Unusually, Tall Bob would not be sitting with his pads on waiting to bat during most of the MAD innings. Instead he would be sitting with his pads off after being out in the second ball of the first over. Chasing 133 to win, The MAD were cruising at 126-2 with several overs in hand. However, the light was starting to fade fast and The MAD wouldn't be The MAD

Webster shows his talents off at football

unless they contrived to make life difficult for themselves. Westmoreland, Shorten, Timms and Smith all failed, leaving just one over remaining and still four runs to get. Cometh the hour, cometh the man and Jake Hotson strode to the crease. He played one shot, a perfectly (and I mean perfectly) timed square cut through the gathering gloom for four. He then strode off again to the applause of his teammates. It was no surprise that it was voted Champagne moment of the season.

In the middle of June the team played the semi-final of the Friendly Cup against Cholsey. Jan Webster avoided the lintel of the Red Lion and indeed the entire game, but nevertheless The MAD won by five wickets, with nine overs to spare after bowling the hosts out for just 125. That was it, we were through to the final, the actual final of an actual ruddy cup competition! Over the coming weeks the team went into a frenzy of imagination of how we were going to celebrate the destined triumph. Thornton Smith was commissioned to construct a mobile trophy cabinet, which could then be carried before the team in the 2017 season much like a Roman Standard. However, the main idea was to hire an open top bus, of which there are plenty in Oxford, which would be adorned with banners produced in Russ's print factory. We would then parade the streets to crowds of bemused tourists as we passed the grounds of our main rivals, principally Isis and Queens College. With victory already assured, we could hardly wait for the September final.

After the euphoria of the semi-final The MAD were very nearly bought back down to earth in the next match, a T20 against… yep, the Isis again. This book would require at least another chapter or maybe even a separate appendix to list the times we've thrown games away from a winning position. Here we went from needing 16 runs off the last 4.4 overs with nine wickets remaining, to still needing five runs off the last five balls.

One guy deserves to be in the photo, the other….

Rather than Jake, fortunately this time it was Dave Shorten who kept his head and his wicket, when several about were losing theirs, to bring the team home with one ball to spare.

On 17th July the team returned to Cholsey for the third time in the season. Since their semi-final defeat Cholsey had been hurting and hurting bad. They had scoured the area for talent and in a local curry house had found a certain Jay Rahman. He was in at three and faced his first ball from Dave Shorten. It was a beautiful ball, pitched on a length, on or around off stump. Jay just leaned into it and pinged it back "like a tracer bullet" to the long off boundary. It was going to be a long afternoon, however at this stage nobody knew just how long. At one point, whilst searching for the ball in an adjacent field, a group of fielders came across a young fox. "Hello fella. There, there, we'll try not to disturb you again." Two balls later: "Hello Mr Fox, maybe this isn't the safest place for you?" Despite being dropped on at least a couple of occasions it was a magnificent innings, 218 not out off 113 balls including 27 fours and a mere 12 sixes. The Far from the MCC were utterly shell shocked and exhausted. Jan then recorded another blob and we slumped to a 174 run defeat.

Late July saw the visit of Hendricks XI, a touring team of Warwick University alumni. A decent bunch who dispensed a bottle of gin to our MOTM. The same week saw Martin

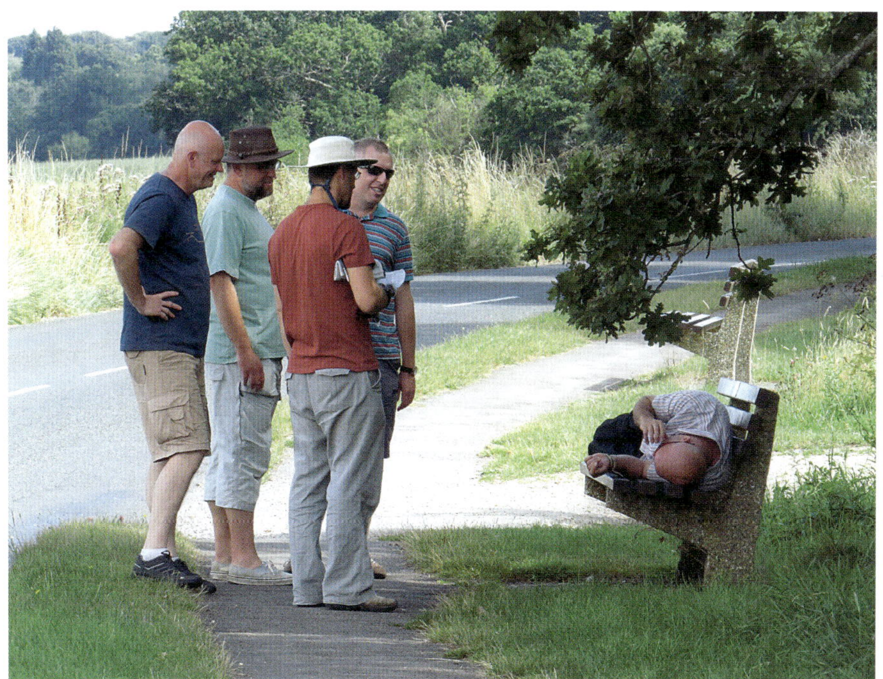

James doing his best to assimilate with the hobos of Hythe

Westmoreland play his trademark one good innings of the season to record 87 off exactly 100 balls during the rollover of Wootton and Bladon.

What is it about R Simpson of Middleton Stoney? Will he ever get bored of flogging The MAD to all parts of a small village north of Oxford? His 52 not out in 18 balls was utterly predictable, but what is a man to do? The man in the spotlight being Howarth, whose first over went for 31 but did at least contain one dot ball.

The previous season's Tour had been such a success (plus no alternatives were forthcoming) that the team decided to return to The Fountain Court Hotel (aka Balti Towers) in Hythe and Dibden for the 2016 Tour. Although it was hard to conceive how, the hotel had actually sunk to further depths in the intervening year. It appeared that the owners had sub-let the bar, thereby handing over responsibility for removing the knuckle dragging regulars who had been banned from everywhere else in the area.

Recovering alcoholic, James Hoskins, causing no issues at the crease with Parkinson

Whenever we mentioned where we were staying to opposition teams, they would roll their eyes and say that they'd been there – once. The hotel did at least have one of those velvet ropes, used to cordon off areas outside nightclubs, and it came in extremely handy to seal off one area of the conference room where Lee Ainsworth had collapsed. It was quite in keeping that Matt Bullock returned to his room on the Saturday night to find a stranger asleep in his bed. An amiable fellow, he had simply blundered upstairs after being refused any more drink and crashed through the first available doorway. That's the stranger, not Matt, boom boom.

We had four great games that year including repeat fixtures against everyone's favourites, Pylewell Park CC and a return against Hythe and Dibden CC who we'd tied with in 2015. For the H&D game, Steve Parkinson drove seven hours from his farm in Lincolnshire, along Friday evening clogged 'A' Roads, to arrive just in time to bat at number 11. He was subsequently run out for five by James Hoskins. A big shout for clubman of the year went to Martin Westmoreland, who had pulled his hamstring the week before. He nevertheless attended the complete four days, put up with Reeves' snoring and didn't take to the pitch once. A true champion.

At the end of August, as the days were getting shorter and the leaves were starting to turn, The MAD travelled to one of their most regular fixtures, the Astons. Russ notched up his second win as Captain to make it two out of two as captain with a 12 run win. The game will forever be remembered because an enterprising carpenter from the Astons had hollowed out a stump to create a stump-cam, which meant the action from the centre could be watched, and recorded, live from the pavilion. A couple of moments are therefore recorded for posterity. First there was Dave Emerson's send-off of Ralph Smith, but of course the main event was the ridiculous dismissal of Andrew Darley (0). Coincidently there was a video doing the rounds on YouTube and later used in an advert, from Bradfield cricket club. Andrew Darley's effort was very similar, a wild swing, a stumble and then a splattering of all three stumps. Thanks for the memory Andrew. The MAD moment award is like an anti-Champagne moment award. It is for the funniest, most incompetent moment of the season. As of 2016 this hall of shame has but one member.

So finally, after months of anticipation it was time for the final of the friendly cup, which surely was to be the highlight of the season. Would the cup have a lid on it, like the FA cup, so some plonker could dance around wearing it? How much do open topped buses cost to hire? I can't comment because I wasn't there, but based on personal accounts and an excellent match report, the OCCSCC were just a little too good, bugger. Yes, there was to be no tickertape parades, no spots in the local paper, no page on The MAD website dedicated to our triumph, just thoughts of what might have been and hopes that 2017 would be our year.

As the world imploded in a swirl of recrimination and regret the final action of 2016 was the AGM, where Lee Ainsworth won Player of the Season for his 572 runs at 44.00 and his 15 wickets at a little under 12. Howarth was also excellent with 641 runs at 42.73, as was Timms who took 38 wickets at under 15. Looking back on 2016, The MAD really had tried their best not to change a thing. We were back in the Blue Room of the St Aldates Tavern, we'd been to the same place on tour, Jake Hotson once again won champagne moment. Sambuca was drunk, but fortunately this time no shoulders were damaged in the arm wrestling. We had at least learnt one lesson. ■

JOHN REED
salad

2017

Ian Howarth

AFTER answering a plea from Captain Timms to make up the numbers, it is doubtful Dave Barlow had any expectations on April 16, other than joining the *Duck on Debut* club and spending the rest of his afternoon retrieving balls from hedgerows, children's play areas and a cycle speedway track. Three years had elapsed since the last pasting at Horspath CC, after which a directive by The MAD committee had been enacted to end these season commencing drubbings and play a softer game elsewhere. However, since *elsewhere* was Cholsey's uncovered bog by an asylum, mostly in the drizzle, the committee revoked its earlier directive, and the team once again visited that picturesque league ground built on healthy membership, youth development and a propensity for nicking local talent. It also helps that their teas are lovely and it's still £2.75 a pint. It's also 50 miles of petrol saved for fixture secretary Howarth.

Perhaps aware of the disparity in recent results, the home side were shorn of a few notable names, but nonetheless good enough to smack 197-6. Nothing new there then, other than the decision to play 35 overs instead of 40 probably saved The MAD chasing 300. In reply, Geoff Carter hit a boundary before joining a small crowd in the pavilion probably thinking "here we go again." Turner (20) was impressive, as he always is compiling no more than 20, before Ainsworth and Howarth made drinks at 67-2. It was only after this partnership continued to blossom and Horspath's bowling became ragged that The MAD suddenly realised they could *actually* win this game. With last year's *Player of the Season* adding a glorious 137 runs for the 3rd wicket with the guy who should have been *Player of the Season* on more than a couple of occasions, it turned out, they could. Oblivious of MAD collapses of yore, Mr Barlow (13*) strode out to bat in the dying overs and hit the winning runs. A delirious Howarth was quoted in the bar afterwards by stipulating "things can only go downhill from here." They did.

Before this prophetic slump in fortunes there was great cause for optimism. Two wholly successful seasons looked like continuing with the re-emergence of Lord Lucan, not the real nanny killer (allegedly), but rather Richard John Bingham Hadfield, whose innings of 72 at the start of the millennia is still a MAD record on debut. This compelling and

Closing in on the implausible nay impossible

scholarly fellow then vanished before reappearing for a duck six years later, since when he's averaged less than three games per season before his brittle mind and body disintegrate. A remarkable MAD season high of 88 on the agricultural minefields of Freeland was followed up with a sublime 65 not out on the impeccable plastic of Enstone. The latter effort part of a wonderful, unbroken partnership of 86 with Mike Reeves to win the game. And then, predictably, he was gone.

In the coming months, there were purported sightings from around the globe of a bespectacled, vertically challenged cricketer, but each time these revelations proved false. There was even a quite ludicrous tale of someone playing under Richard's name for the Bodleian, but this was assumed a very bad joke. Wherever he went, whatever he was doing, whoever he was bludgeoning to death in a basement, word eventually got to Mr Hadfield that he needed *five* innings to qualify for the end of season MAD handbook. He duly reappeared for the final game of the season to be run out for one in front of his parents.

Tom Crowe's merry bunch of mercenaries can be spotted on most of the village greens in Oxford. Hailing from a sewerage plant in Appleton, they travel far and wide to make sure The MAD get a damned good shoeing at weekends, and if time allows, they'll rock up at a midweek T20 for good measure. One of their favourite *other* clubs is Wootton & Boars Hill, a delightful little ground atop a hill boasting panoramic views of fields that tumble off into the distance. For it was here, after Andrew Darley's scintillating spell of bowling (8-3-20-4) that this hybrid band of legionnaires really began to shine. Mr Glover (87*) is Wootton through and through, with allegiances to Appleton of course. Then there is the long haired Bill Webb (36), if you can imagine a cultured and artistic Captain Caveman. Oh, he's *definitely* from that aloof little parish on the way to Swindon. Well, by incorporating a landing site for the ball in nearby paddocks, this apple-tasting *lower order* tonked 171 from the final 22 overs. Game over. It wasn't all doom and gloom of course, the sun shone brightly during much of the run riot, several *rested* MAD players took the opportunity to laugh at the massacre, and of course Mr Timms hit a personal best of 45 as the home team gave up trying.

They say you shouldn't dance around people's graves, and in an odd quirk of fate The MAD gained revenge in a Wednesday slogathon a few weeks later. A quirk of many T20s is the retirement rule, some enforce it and some don't. The St Clement Strollers didn't used to, they enjoyed sitting back watching balls sail into a nearby mosque as Mr Higgs raised his bat on reaching three figures. Utterly pointless in my humble opinion, particularly if you have a bunch of youngsters sat on their arses with nothing better to do. Many teams retire you at 30, some at the end of the over you reach 30, some at 50 and one at 42†.

It is doubtful retirement made a huge difference to the outcome of this match on a hot summer's evening, then again, maybe it did? Wootton's Mr Collins was going great guns before being shouted he was to retire at the end of the over, he was subsequently

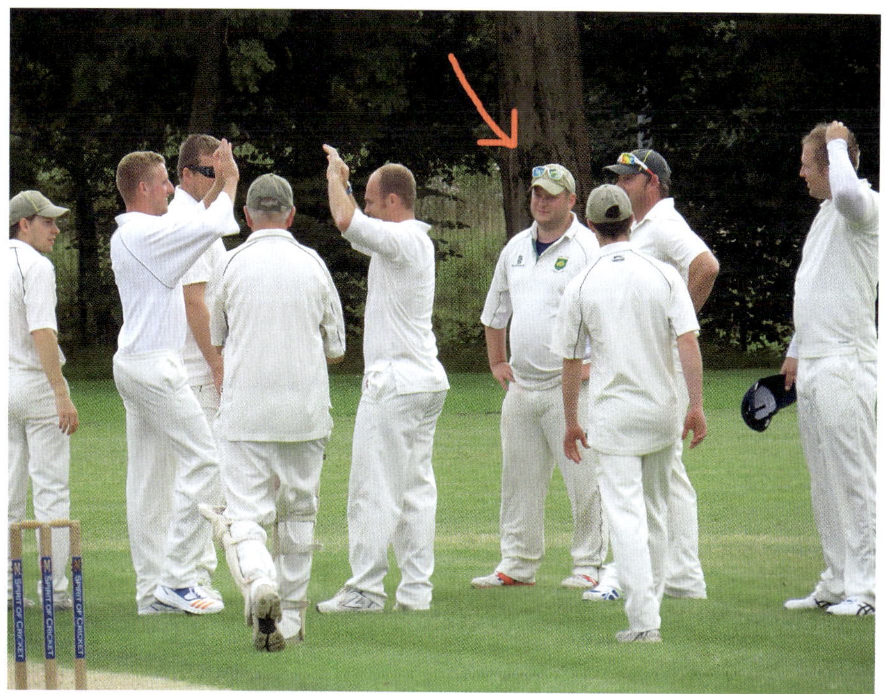

Serial hater of all things MAD, Tom Crowe

† Warwick University graduates Hendrick's XI have an obsession with 42, a number derived from The Hitchhiker's Guide to the Galaxy, where a super computer decided this was the answer to life, the universe and everything. These disciples of Douglas Adam's wildly bonkers books also have an obsession with gin, hence their name.

bowled. The aforementioned Webb (31*) and Ulyatt (36*) got there in the final over, so for them it didn't matter. It mattered for Dave Shorten (33*), who watched his team collapse after dragging his cudgel dolefully from the pitch, but not Mr Ainsworth (30), who after resurrecting the run chase wasn't told to retire (The MAD geniuses doing the scoring and those leaning over the book apparently couldn't add up to thirty). As it was, it mattered little, Lee was run out in the next and final over having been Mr Pearson's running bitch throughout. A wonderful last ball victory was secured after James' new running bitch, Jake Hotson, covered all twenty two yards to far greater success.

As with the pyrotechnics of Mr Glover mentioned earlier, one man can often be the defining difference between two teams. Throughout 2017, it felt as though there was an endless queue of these *batting bullies* all jostling for position to open their shoulders, grab the game by the scruff of its neck and give The MAD a resolute thrashing. Next up was Mr Bollig, a man of no great build, but of obvious cricketing pedigree. Arriving fashionably late at Oriel for the game against OUP, he played himself in for seven balls at number six before raising eyebrows by launching James Hoskins into an adjacent college. These eyebrows were soon complemented with open mouths as a total of 22 boundaries flew off his bat, his 125 not out off just 57 balls containing several deliveries which were seen no more.

Even after the Bollig barrage the wheels hadn't totally come off The MAD bus, victory in the dystopian nothingness of Kilkenny against Wootton & Bladon followed a rousing first round victory in the Friendly Cup over Cholsey. The latter will perhaps be remembered not for Howarth and Shorten's 73 run partnership, but for Geoff Carter's 47 ball innings of… erm, three. You could argue he laid the foundations for the run chase, you could *also* argue he was concreted into the sodding foundations. So inept and visually impaired was this innings, some of the opposition were left wondering where

Chaos outside the asylum….

he'd left his white cane and labradoodle. Other fantastic memories of this match were the chaos of a Levi's-wearing Westmoreland running for a now injured Dave Shorten, and Thornton Smith being shouted back to the pavilion after walking out with a broken bat. We live for these moments, such like that of Polly Moon's debut in a T20 at the postcard perfect Cumnor, remaining unbeaten on one not out after her fiancé Mr Hoskins was castled for a golden duck. James would later pick himself up, backpedal on the boundary to catch the Bodleian's G. A. Robinson's final shot in anger.

It is said you never lose as long as you learn, but from June 7th until August 11th the Far from the MCC lost a hell of a lot and didn't learn a damned thing. During this period of seismic underachievement there were a staggering sixteen defeats, one of which (whisper it quietly) was by a single run to the (ahem) Bodleian. Among these forgettable results posted with a red "L" on the website, a few more of these *batting bullies* would come to the fore.

Accommodating touring teams whenever possible, The MAD hosted a talented Battisford CC at the University Club in town. Agriculturalist Norfolk pissheads by trade, it was decided a pre-match pub crawl might narrow the contrasting skill sets. It didn't. Foremost was farmer C Bull clubbing twenty boundaries on his way to 100 (retired drunk) off balls unknown due to a barely decipherable scorebook. This Saturday hammering, part of a double-header, would also mark the debut of the unassuming Cornelius Johannes Vermaak. At odds with Spitting Image's satirical song deriding South Africans, it is impossible to comprehend quite what this endearing, sober house flipper from Witbank was thinking, exposed to a tidal wave of booze, as balls vanished between dreamy spires after taking out Oxford gargoyles on route. A partially reversed, but utterly slaughtered BCC batting line-up would end up smashing 283 off just 33.3 overs. No, Corne *didn't* get a duck, and no we didn't chase it down, even when the league toppers generously bowled with their wrong arm and hardly bothered moving for the ball.

This obliteration of the senses was the tune-up for the following day's visitation of those unconquerable Lemmings, with their ten bodies being infinitely superior and undoubtedly more sagacious to The MAD's old-school eleven. After Reeves (44*) and Bullock (20) had rescued The MAD innings from a parlous 59-7, 137 would have seemed a distant ask for the ex-university boys (stumbling on 31-3). They needn't have worried however, as one of five Baker's on show, Matt simply rolled up his sleeves to pound 67 not out, including two enormous sixes that smashed home team hopes and a few roofing slates to boot. As this book goes to press, this club has still *never* beaten the smug Lemmings in fourteen times of trying. How they must gloat, and how we'll be monitoring their Facebooks….

An awful evening's pasting by *that* sewerage works would precede the rampant destruction by *Bully Boy #4*, or is that *#5*? After contesting last year's final in the Friendly Cup, hopes were high that The MAD could go one stage further and actually win something to put in that non-existent trophy cabinet in our non-existent pub. On a sweltering afternoon in mid-June, these dreams and aspirations evaporated into the Stanton St John's turf as Mr R. Stephenson belted 115 in an insurmountable Isis total of 235. Temperatures were so high during this fortnight that Hoskins collapsed with double vision whilst umpiring and cameras failed to work during a T20 in Islip, although one suspects a brief read of the user manual might have been to the benefit of Mr Shorten.

With players unavailable due to family commitments and overseas holidays†, The MAD would find themselves temporarily light in numbers during the aforementioned heatwave. The *not-to-be-pronounced-when-drunk* Srinivasan Janarthanan and young Daniel Ron Shaw would guest during another OUP clobbering at Jesus College, before the eternal wait for Christopher Trevor John Williams to join MAD ranks would end at Harwell International. A batsman of considerable calibre, 'Pops' had been on the club's radar for many years, ever since the Sunday OU Offices imploded and all his 'mates' buggered off to play for The MAD. His father Trevor used to run the Wayfarers, a spirited and distinguished team formed in 1949 in the wages department of Morris Motors. Alas the team folded with Williams Snr no longer able or willing to shoulder the burden alone. With nowhere left to play and no end to the perpetual nagging both at work and down the pub, the engaging and dependable Williams Jnr finally put pen to paper, signing off on his image rights and loyalty bonus he became MAD player #144.

The game in Harwell was memorable for many reasons. Chris (8) failed to bag a duck on debut and played against himself (Harwell fielded their own C Williams), Russ Turner (57) finally discovered the middle of his bat and one of the opposition batsmen

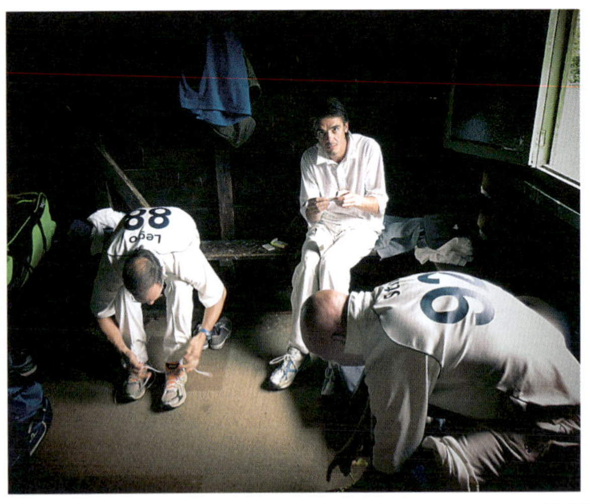

Mr Williams wondering why someone is stalking the changing room with a camera

† *The irony of this author hiding in the shade of Greek olive trees on the island of Paxos at the time isn't lost on me.*

stood his ground after twice edging behind. The naming confusion would later persist with first change bowler J Timms flummoxing skipper and scorer G Timms (spelling your own name can be tough), and that of his lovely scoring companion Corde, who found similar confusion when penning Corne (Vermaak). The red faced chuntering of the miserly Newman-Robson (8-1-22-2) would alas be to no avail, The MAD lost.

Inbetween some more arbitrary defeats going into July, the weather took a decidedly more English downturn with the games against Iffley Village and Islip abandoned. The first was pure common sense, the second beggared belief, that both pouring rain and horrific weather apps couldn't lure the opposition back inside. It was both sad and perplexing watching from afar as the Brasenose covers were sloshed back and forth in between the deluges, as gaggles of men in soggy whites discussed the plainly bloody ludicrous. The real annoyance was our *borrowed* scorebook left soaking up the rain.

However some games weren't lost to the elements, the blame for *their* non-occurrence lies with modern society. Many adults now work weekends and some wives and girlfriends actually demand their husband's time (or *quality time* depending on your predilection). The kids have way too many options these days too, if it isn't motocross, basketball or tee-ball, then they're sat on their arses with an Xbox blasting zombies into outer space. And whilst I'm on this growing tirade, Oxford even has adolescents cavorting about with broomsticks between their legs playing f______ Quidditch! This embarrassing, nonsensical idiocy with multiple quaffles (deflated volleyballs) and someone called a *snitch* legging it about with a sock and tennis ball hanging out their arse was derived from a Harry Potter novel no less. I'm not even sure the celebrated J. K. Rowling could bear to watch this pathetically depressing homage to her literary talent. With *so* many distractions and so many obligations the village cricket we all know and love is slowly dying.

Is this really a sport...?

Founded in 1872, Wallingford were once a thriving league club with two decent teams, then one, then they merged with Blewbury & Upton who boasted a brand new pavilion funded by the parish council. With dwindling interest this joint enterprise is sadly no more, with Nigel Walter doing his damndest to maintain a motley crew for a midweek bash. Garsington had three teams, yet Simon Goves had to cancel as they now have none. Former opponents Hanney have perished too, whilst others such as Great & Little Tew, Swinbrook and Chearsley continue to struggle manfully. Now the only legacies of some of these once proud little clubs are abandoned grounds slowly turning to weed. Factor in a dearth of council sponsored facilities and enthusiasm and the future looks bleak. We'll come back to the council later.

After what seemed an interminable wait, the club suddenly arrived at that Holy Grail in the MAD calendar. Returning to the picturesque harbour town of Minehead after more than a decade, Tour was as edifying as it was gloriously enjoyable, particularly if you disregarded the results. Bewildered that Dave Shorten had somehow booked sixteen drunkards in a top hotel for hostel prices, Thursday became an enduring odyssey to Stogumber by foot and a Somerset steam train. The wonderful surrounds of a hilltop ground were at odds with Captain Darley's grotesque batting order, but a game of some purpose was rescued by the aforementioned Shorten smashing 20 not out at number eleven (a MAD record). His cameo wasn't the only thing to delight, with a weekend

Mike Ashley draining a whole cock

Wurzels' gig leaving barrels of knockoff scrumpy in its wake. A Sambuca fuelled orgy of excess the following night followed an entertaining T20 against Minehead CC. Set an implausible 142 for victory, Russ Turner survived on 17 not out but not before he was likened to Sports Direct's Mike Ashley. Some names just stick. He certainly drank like the Newcastle United supremo.

With hangovers being slept off in skittle alleys and players suffering the effects of carbon monoxide poisoning on a hired bus transfer, Saturday night's de facto curry night would postdate the not insubstantial thrashing from the youthful L Trottman. To call this sharp cut, spindly blonde upstart a *bully* seems harsh, he was no higher than a privet hedge, but could whack a ball higher than a redwood. Before his slightly disappointing retirement on 102*, the twelve monstrous sixes he clubbed had Newman-Robson crying in his sticker-adorned coffin and the wedding primed Pearson stationed permanently in an adjacent field.

The gorgeous Bridgetown ground

A marvellous celebration of who we are was bookended at quite possibly one of the prettiest and most idiosyncratic grounds we've ever played at. Accessed by a wooden bridge over the river Exe, the bucolic charms of Bridgetown CC are symbolised by a thatched pavilion clinging daringly to a far bank which looked down on sloping boundaries to its right. With an unspoken decree to bash the ball into the river, fielders and spectators alike are joined by excited kids in a race to net the ball back to land. It really was a crazy, timeless experience for all. Mr Ainsworth's continued form and 59 with the bat were ultimately futile however, but this day belonged to the village of Bridgetown and all those that made it happen, including the balls you chased uphill that then rolled back past you. All four of these Somerset clubs will be warmly welcomed to Oxford should ever they tour.

After the euphoria of Somerset, it was back to the mundane realisation that one needs to work for a living, or at least join the depressing queues of the downtrodden for a jobseekers allowance. There was some cheer however, with James Hoskins vying for his *first* career five-for on the smelliest stage of all. Having run through Appleton's top order with an assortment of flan and darts, he had over two overs with which to finally realise his dream. Predictably he failed (8-0-33-4) and predictably The MAD lost and predictably Ainsworth (54) was the only telling contributor with the bat. Unpredictably the hosts dragged everyone back to The Eight Bells in Eaton afterwards to survey wealthy ladies in heels sporting freshly styled cuts and false tits.

James Pearson got married to the lovely Fionnuala on the weekend of August 20, and in doing so selfishly deprived the team of players for the trip to Didcot CC. So much so, an ungoverned and chiefly patchwork ensemble was hastily glued together by Howarth on the morning of the match, bitter memories of yore coming flooding back. Perhaps still paralytic from the nuptial celebrations above, Dave Emerson shocked all by agreeing to play, and having certified himself incapable of movement at slip, duly scampered 34 not out for a four wicket win. The victory was a much needed shot of adrenalin, however the formula was clearly heroin as evidenced from the tonking off R. A. Smith's bat the following week. Ralph's innings of exactly 100 was two runs better than that he scored for Astons earlier in the season, caught on the boundary by Westmoreland in the mistaken belief he'd already reached his milestone. Begrudgingly however, this was a super innings from *Bully Boy #7* and probably his finest to date, and at no point did his dad do any umpiring and turn a plumb LBW down.

With weather curtailing any hopes of a third place finish in the Friendly Cup, a long and arduous season suddenly came to its soggy conclusion on September 10. Injudicious shot selection and poor bowling can leave their scars, but nothing comes close to the psychological damage wrought by the ineptitude of the Oxford County Council. This was the fifth game of the season at Cutteslowe Park and the *fifth* game running they screwed it up. For others cricket simply means rocking up with a can of beer and a kitbag, for Mr Reeves and myself, the innocent and angelic Kathy was the *only* reason one of us didn't have a serious meltdown and take a bat to that hidden council office. Wrong keys, wrong dates, wrong times, wrong invoices and double booked pavilions only begin to tell the sorry tale, but changing into my whites in the confines of a smelly public toilet will live long.

The game itself ended in a 4 run victory over our neighbours and nemesis, Isis CC. A match notable for Jan Webster hitting a personal high of 30 for The MAD, but in doing so sawing off Hadfield and having his bicycle nicked. Howarth (39*) and Turner (25*) would finally discover they could bat, whilst 'Pops' Williams stole the comedic headlines by casually rolling up his sleeves as he sauntered airily under a sitter, organising his hair and makeup and then dropping the bloody thing. With rain now tumbling from the heavens, all that was left to do was shake hands and agree to reunite at the AGM, and *of course* fight a losing battle whilst attempting to lock those godawful pavilion doors.

Hadfield and Webster discussing their respective views on the laws governing being run out

At the aforementioned piss-up, heavy drinking and missed postal votes saw to it that the Player of the Season was James Hoskins for his 37 wickets at 17.78. His consummate artistry in the bakery saw off Lee Ainsworth's 565 runs at 35.21, his five fifties and also his 15 wickets at 15.93. Both had excellent seasons much like Mike Reeves, whose rewards for bowling more overs than anyone else (127.2), hitting more runs than he'd ever done (379), and starring in some match winnings partnerships himself (86* with R. J. B. Hadfield at Enstone) was to poll as many votes as Steve Parkinson on the night. Steve of course didn't play a single game but did look assured at the bar. Lee's bad luck was however tempered by receiving the Ade Fisher Performance Trophy in combination with Howarth, for that wonderful partnership in that particular match where this whole chapter started some 4,000 words ago. He also bagged the Fantasy winnings before spraying champagne all over the St Aldates Tavern for his running catch on the boundary at Stogumber. ■

EPILOGUE

ONLY an *incredibly* optimistic Edmund Neil Lester could have envisaged that the ragtag bunch of guys he pulled together to form a cricket club would still be in existence today. Backed by hard Irish pounds from the whimsical Noel Reilly two decades ago, our posthumous patron and landlord of all things Thomas Hardy, this pub team with no pub chalked off their 444th career match at the end of this season. In a strange quirk of fate, the game against Isis was contested where it all started at Cutteslowe Park, presumably with better officialdom, but maybe not.

The barometer for any cricket club's health can be derived by the volume of its membership and enthusiasm. In that respect the Far from the MCC are currently in wonderful shape, never better with Skipper Timms able to utilise twenty different faces in the season's opening fortnight alone, and with a committee of seven able bodies willing to muck out the stable, things continue to bowl along just fine.

It has been an honour and privilege for both Mike and myself to try and ape the literary skills of Mr A. G. Mann, an impossible ask by our own admission. Attempting to summarise the last nine years of all things MAD, we've attempted to capture an essence of everyone and everything. Our eternal thanks to all who have contributed with their revelations, facts and forgotten memories, I just hope we've managed a half decent job and in a way that does this great club proud.

Here's to the next decade or two. See you on the field or in the pub. ■

Lord Lucan
13

Contents: Part 2

A Bodleian Perspective

Stuart Guy Ackland
Player #131

WRITE something about The MAD's, says Spam, from the perspective of an outsider. What to write? About the numerous changes in name and location, the amount of drinking, the often bewildering names on the backs of the shirts? How, on the first time of playing for them, the skipper drops two sitters off your bowling?

A brief history of MAD / Bodleian combat. Our first game was on the 24th of June 2001, when the Bodleian took on Jude the Obscure at Pembroke College. Lovely ground, dodgy car-park. An incomplete scorebook still manages to show some familiar names; Antony Mann, both Mander's (Tony and Ben), Jake Hotson, Matt Bullock, Thornton Smith and Ade Fisher. Jude win by 7, the start of a number of seasons of results going back and forth until a long spell of MAD victories with an occasional Bodley win. Tony Mander has a special place in shared history, scoring the winning runs *for* the Bodleian in 2004, which was maybe a bad thing as we didn't taste success again for a number of years, the nadir being a 10 wicket defeat at that most soulless of grounds, Stratfield Brake, in 2007. Ant Mann being good friends with our own Andy MacKinnon was the reason for the fixtures; Andy still plays for the Bodleian while Ant has gone south for sun and familiar accents. Despite the occasional one-sided thrashings that have been handed out by one or the other, it's a sign of a respect and friendship that has grown over the years, though desperation on the day has a lot to do with it as well. Both teams have had to call on players from the other side to make up an 11 on a Sunday afternoon.

Ultimately the thing to write about is the obvious camaraderie on and off the pitch, an enviable friendship and all-for-one spirit that is apparent in the piss-taking, the acceptance of fines post-match, the drinking both *before* and after the game and in the continual willing rotation of umpires and all the other jobs that need to be done. It is this friendship that creates a team. They're also good at playing the game as well. Bastards.

'Course, the ultimate irony is that long after the teams have folded due to old age and shagged kneecaps, this book will survive, deep in the vaults of the Bodleian, taunting all the ex-Bod CC'ers with its shiny cover, stats and reports of matches long since played out. Bodley produced their own books for the first ten years of playing, poor efforts called *The Finger,* produced in house with a colour photo-copier and blue-tack, nothing compared to a properly published effort with an ISBN and all. Our only hope is, what with over 10,000,000 books to choose from, this will soon be forgotten. If not we can always put it in the wrong place, losing it forever.... ■

Notes of Wootton & Bladon C.C.

Derek Hambridge

THE first time that I had any contact with the FFTMCC was some ten years ago when I started doing the scoring for our cricket club on Sunday afternoons.

It was an away match at one of the Oxford college grounds. Oxford college grounds are known for the quality of the wicket that is prepared for any match.

Our bowlers were delighted to be playing on a wicket that they thought would show off their collective skills.

The ground was carefully hidden away the wrong side of the main railway line going south from Oxford. Fortunately there was a long foot bridge over the tracks, quite handy if you were carrying a full cricket bag.

While I was preparing the scorebook the teams were out doing a little catching practice. It was then I first noticed the numbers and hieroglyphics on the backs of the FFTMCC shirts. It was the first time I had seen numbers on shirts.

The shirts themselves were obviously treasured by their owners, from pristine white and through the spectrum to something less than white. It also looked as if the club iron had not been passed around quite quickly enough during the week.

So there was this slightly dishevelled team doing catching practice in front of me when I realised two additional facts. The shirt numbering system was hardly uniform and they could all catch a ball.

Scoring was easier than I thought after I had written down all the team shirt numbers. It is a random numbering system that a cryptographer would have delighted in.

Their openers played as if they knew the wicket was not hiding any idiosyncrasies, steadily amassing the runs, hitting through the V and not nicking anything. As the cream of our bowling attack began to toil the openers changed tactics and started hitting the ball harder and were rewarded with boundaries. I pencilled in "can bat a bit" next to the openers names for future reference.

Our skip changed bowlers and the old heads on less than fit shoulders who could give the ball a good tweak soon had three back in the pavilion giving the scoreboard an air of respectability. By tea the total favoured the FFTMCC but not as much as I first thought it might.

After tea with a decent total set our batting would need to be inspired. So it was but whenever I thought we might get this our trademark middle order collapse intervened and we ended up snatching defeat from the jaws of victory.

That over the years has been pretty much the random pattern of our matches, first one side then the other.

When FFTMCC changed to another college ground we thought that we might have a run of victories to mull over in the pub opposite their ground. The random pattern of results has been kept up. Rather like El Nino which also reverses at will.

The delightful thing about playing the FFTMCC is the friendship that has built up over the years between the core of each team.

Collectively they are knowledgeable about the game, good competitors, fair, play for each other and like all good Sunday sides a touch quirky and great fun to play each season.

The real winner in all of our matches has been the weather. To say that it has been less than clement on the majority of occasions is a fact.

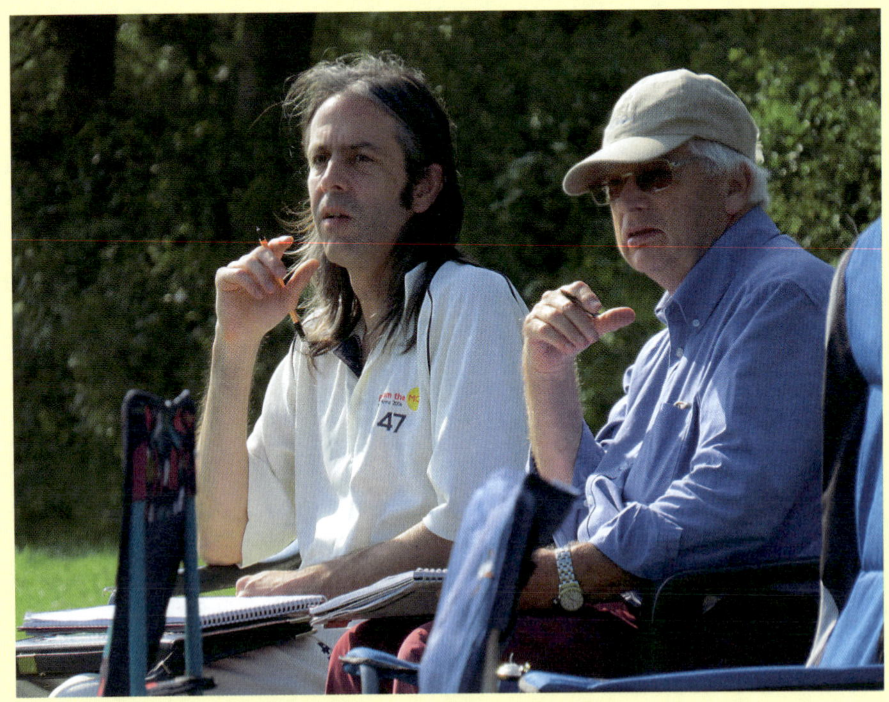

Me with some druid on scoring duty

Meticulous preparations are needed to score at our fixtures. Umbrellas, paperweights, several sheets of industrial grade polythene, hand warmers and a heavy raincoat usually worn by Ozzie stockmen in the wet season.

I have seen the poor souls who have been out in the middle doing their ten overs of umpiring coming back blue with cold, wet and a fifty fifty chance that a pulse is still present.

I have always attributed the dubious LBW decisions down to restricted blood supply to the brain in such conditions.

On the few balmy days when the same thing happens we are back to dubious eyesight bought on by that fifth pint of larger from the night before or a modest deficit of understanding relating to the current documentation on the LBW law… let's not go there.

All Sunday cricketers are blessed with an encyclopaedic knowledge of the laws and far more importantly their batting and bowling averages at any given moment in the season down to three decimal places.

All of which makes for good banter between the teams at the local waterhole after the match.

Over the years I have looked for a common denominator that keeps such an eclectic bunch of soul's together year in year out.

It is the love of the game.

Play them if you can you will not be disappointed. ■

MAD Player Profiles

Gary Timms

Matt Bullock #018

Being the oldest serving member of the Far from the MCC, Matt's seen the lot. As the years have ebbed by, he's witnessed denims and doc martens replaced by whites and shiny spikes. He's seen the club rise from the dead, move home, rebrand, move home and rebrand again. He's captained the team, toured all over the UK with them, and chaired two decades of 'MAD' AGM's. He's filed the scorebooks, updated the records and written onto paper things ineffaceable. Moreover, Matt has had countless banter with nearly *all* of the 144 other lads and lasses who have at one time or another stood in a field with him on a Sunday or some dreamy summer evening. In short, Matthew is The MAD.

Intelligent, oracular and quick witted in equal measure, the team have always presented a more rounded and wholesome feel with his presence – especially at the bar. The salient Matt Bullock has improved with age, with 2017 underscoring him as the club's *Most Improved Player*. This wasn't the result of a pissed vote at the AGM, it was based on the fact he almost took as many wickets in one season as he had in the past nineteen. He can also boast achieving the pinnacle of Sunday Cricket by catching onetime 'Wisden Cricketer of the Year', former England opening bat Claire Taylor.

Captain's comparison – Shane Warne; the leggies, the 'fast' cars, the occasional splurge with the bat, the beer, the women…

James Hoskins #027

JMO is a MAD institution. He has devoted over a third of his life to this Club and has never asked for anything in return, other than being ignored when he asks to be pushed up the batting order. Relentlessly positive, energetic and fantastically eccentric, Mr Hoskins has done it all having first been spotted by a boundary drinking Stella all those years ago. Since then, that intuitive nature saw him Skipper the team and has allowed him to bag more wickets than anyone in MAD history with his mastery of all things pie.

It's not always been plain sailing for James however. A few years ago, he left his team mates in the shit to go on some ridiculous, life-affirming sabbatical around the globe. On this trip, he did some stuff, took a bunch of photos and met some bird in his selfish pursuit of inner harmony. Of course the money dried up, as it does and JMO returned to the UK to screw over telecommunications giants working as a mercenary contractor.

Captain's comparison – Hanse Cronje; a leader, a captain, an all-rounder, a "gambler".

Jake Hotson #047

Dry, acerbic and resolutely anti-establishment, Jake's debut for The MAD can be traced right back to the millennium, where he was lucky enough to play in the club's first official Cup game (a resolute tonking against Stokenchurch CC). In crushing defeat, he immediately embraced the sarcastic, disjointed drunks masquerading as team mates and signed up for more. He's still here of course, salivating for another helping each year, albeit in slightly more talented company. Mr Hotson has dedicated *over a third* of his life to this Club, and never once turned up on time or had his hair cut.

A deeply intelligent soul, Jake likes nothing better than advanced compound algebraic calculations, deeply coded web design, zany music compilations and directing tirades of abuse at 21st century society and Tory politicians. He's also well versed with a proper good moan – particularly regarding Oxford beer prices and the fascist landlords who kick him out at closing time.

Captain's comparison – Jack Russell; Looks like Jack. Keeps like Jack. Bats with the tenacity of Jack. Is it Jack?

Richard Hadfield #050

Whimsical, intelligent, mysterious and purely fictional, the enchanting Mr R. J. B. Hadfield doesn't really exist. Someone assuming that preposterous name at the turn of the millennium notched 72 runs on debut, but vanished soon after. Almost forgotten, another chap purporting to be him finally returned for a duck six years later. Since that day, it seems almost fashionable for vertically challenged, bespectacled cricketers with no real club or association to play under the name of Hadfield when the FFTMCC are short. They are all rather handy with the bat.

These assortments of charismatic, scholarly characters have all proved likeably witty over the years, just a shame none of them have ever really integrated. However, for the eagle-eyed, they do occasionally turn up at the odd AGM to chin a few ales and make hollow boasts about getting more involved. That said, the last *guest* Hadfield had the audacity and sheer front to try recruiting for the Bodleian…

Captain's comparison – Mark Ramprakash; has the effortlessness of Mahela Jayawardene but Mahela played loads at the 'top level'. Ramps not so much. Happy to step down to a lower level though.

Steve Dobner #056

Every club has one – a genocidal, human hand grenade. Since his debut well over a decade ago, the portentous Mr Dobner has managed to have a go at everything and everybody in that time, including himself. However, advancing years and family life have mellowed the inner anger, a cynical and sarcastic mouth replacing the fists and vitriol. Twinkle now finds regular pleasure in his foldback chair, watching with delight as his two girls punch his teammates in the scrotum and smack cricket bats around their heads. They say fruit never falls far from the tree.

Despite his continued existence bullying kids at school in the Land of the White Stiletto, Steve still finds an excuse to travel to Oxford and dish out sarcastic putdowns. The sardonic rapport is infectious, the cricket is fleeting. Where once he could lay claim to being the club's premier all-rounder, now we wonder if he's wearing the right glasses.

Captain's comparison – Matt Prior; more than solid stats belie a player oft perceived a level down from where he really was/is. Normally taken to the brink of breakdown by "team-mates" on tour.

Thornton Smith #057

Capricious, idiosyncratic and comical, the maverick and loquacious Mr Smith has been a beating heart of The Club since the early days when The Jude *were* The MAD. He is a loyal and trustworthy friend, a great man in a tight corner and would do anything for you in times of need. At the same time, he realises that is no reason to be spared from essential piss-taking and withering barbs. He is also a man of a million different business enterprises, specialising in everything wood from fencing to cabinet making, shelving and door hanging, interior and exterior decorating and a complete recreation of the Death Star in seasoned oak. Such is his diversity he'll turn his hand to pretty much anything, apart from some sign-writing on that little white works van of his.

A classically wired contradiction in terms, 410's alternative take on cricket has seen his Skippers increasingly turn to his bowling in recent times. He can bat too, of course he can, but lately he's been much more successful bowling pissed beamers than executing pissed cover drives.

Captain's comparison – Any current West Indian cricketer; talented at all facets of the game but you sort of feel they'd rather be doing anything else.

Nick Hebbes #071

Nick was one of a clutch of new faces that breathed life into The MAD back in 2003. A gifted cricketer with a tirelessly and irritatingly happy persona, his consistently

upbeat personality was in stark contrast to that of his downtrodden, pessimistic team mates. Ever the joker, he was always at the fore of things on Tour, annoying everyone with his astute visual jokes and insane fucking happiness. And don't even mention those stupid plastic singing swords… And then, quite inscrutably, he was gone…

As the years ticked by The Club received occasional emails from someone using his name, but by and large it was understood he was now living elsewhere on Mother Earth as a doting dad. And then it happened, out of the blue, he *mysteriously* reappeared – back in Cholsey – like NOTHING had ever happened…Was it *really* him? Erm, yes… it took all of two minutes for him to take the stereo off pause and go into a diatribe of observational nonsense for anyone who would listen.

Captain's comparison – Danny Morrison; eh, he (was?) a player and not just a commentator?! Well I never.

Martin Westmoreland #072

Forthright and sardonic, Martin's keen sense of wit helps to soften his hard-northern edges. He is considered by his peers to be a cornerstone of The MAD, a key and instrumental figure who helped breathe life into an ale (ing) pub team. At one point or another, Mooman has done everything, so only right that someone regarded as the scrupulous definition of a *true* Clubman is now the Director of Cricket – a hallowed Committee position bestowed on someone who does naff all, other than order some new hoodies.

Along with several other unnamed top order batsmen, Martin largely lives off former glories, though at least he can boast to usually being the guy who smacks the MAD high score for the season. But why bother? He's a bowler of course, as proven by the fact he topped the 2017 bowling averages at a ridiculous 8.88 and never once asked the captains WTF he was so underbowled…

Captain's comparison - Paul Collingwood; handy with bat, under-bowled, catches everything, has retired, right?

Ian Howarth
#077

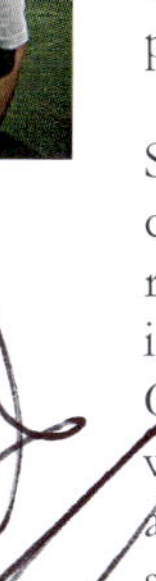

Cynical, sarcastic and tirelessly ebullient, Ian was another member of the Class of '03 that helped breathe life into an ailing pub team. Fractious and ready around his northern edges, he quickly felt at home around his hedonistic team mates and has somehow dealt with Sunday hangovers to plunder all those runs. Forthright and decidedly right when utterly wrong, Spam has overseen two tenures as MAD Skipper, with both incarnations ending in unhappy resignations. A price of passion or simply a troubled mind and soul?

Spam's continued enthusiasm for ALL things MAD has continued unabated over the past decade, being responsible for most of the crap on the website and the intolerable season after season fixture congestion. Criticism that his last worthwhile accolade *on* the pitch was celebrated in sepia, he was lucky enough to be stood at the other end with Ainsworth in 2017, helping to scoop the *Ade Fisher Performance* award at Horspath.

Captain's comparison – Kevin Pietersen; belligerent egotist who bats number 4 and thinks he should bowl more.

Geoff Carter
#089

Quirky, affable, jocular and increasingly schizophrenic, Geoff has been in and around the team's edges for over a decade, and is now regarded as a MAD institution. A carpenter by trade, he enjoys splitting his time between wood, boozing and living the life of a maverick sailor on the Oxford canals. A celebrated opener and tail ender, Geoff knows no other positions in the batting order other than #1 and #11.

Rumoured to occasionally play a shot, he crushes the opposition under a tidal wave of boredom, often mimicking a man with a guide dog out in the middle. He can also keep wicket or at least he can stand behind the stumps with some pads on. Geoff once took a wicket.

Captain's comparison – Michael Atherton & Steve Finn; bats like the Watford Wall and bowls like Athers.

Mike Reeves #093

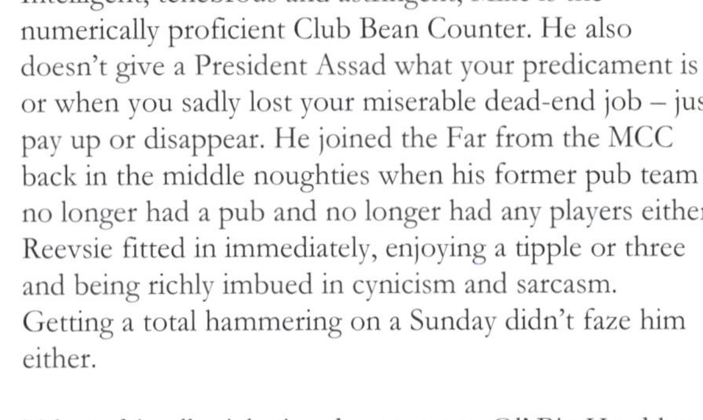

Intelligent, tenebrous and astringent, Mike is the numerically proficient Club Bean Counter. He also doesn't give a President Assad what your predicament is or when you sadly lost your miserable dead-end job – just pay up or disappear. He joined the Far from the MCC back in the middle noughties when his former pub team no longer had a pub and no longer had any players either. Reevsie fitted in immediately, enjoying a tipple or three and being richly imbued in cynicism and sarcasm. Getting a total hammering on a Sunday didn't faze him either.

Talented in all cricketing departments, Ol' Big Head has proved himself reminiscent of a fine wine in recent years, seemingly get better with age. He finally received recognition of this fact by scooping a long overdue POTS award in 2013, banishing the bitter memories of years gone by where his dreams were trampled afoot by those less deserving, but somehow more popular.

Captain's comparison – Mohammad Amir; left arm over swing bowling complimented by lower order (currently) tonking. Financially misguided by others.

Steve Parkinson #094

Caustic and trenchant, Parky the Lincoln hypochondriac is a living paradox. An outstanding gentlemanly exterior is forever fighting the unruly yob within, or is it the other way around? A man of consistently humourous and shockingly dry, intellectual barbs, Steve has always had a magnetic aura about him. Born into a farming community, he honed that aloof and risible arrogance from his time spent in France. That veneer was tarnished soon after joining The MAD however, following several displays of pique and bat throwing that left the rebel rousers drooling at the mouth.

He says fatherhood has smoothed his edges, we beg to differ. Shake Steve's hand and that contemptuous sneer we all love will be betrayed by his eyes. When he isn't plagued by mental or physical injury – which doesn't equate to too many days in the social calendar – Mincer represents a more than handy cricketer. Accurate medium pace (mincing) bowling complementing a dangerous middle order batsman.

Captain's comparison – Quintin De Kock; gifted cricketer with a usually unassuming character. Make him angry and he'll bad mouth your wife though.

Dave Shorten #096

One of life's true good guys. Lego, as he's affectionately known, is the only MAD member to own their own woodland. During his time with the Mad, Dave has broken the record for both the longest and shortest time taken to write a Match Report, enlisted his teammates in a doomed 5-a-side competition, organised a winter fitness regime with the army, and launched his own book; 'A Winner's Guide to Poker'. In short, Mr Shorten is an archetypal example of that perfectly eccentric, amicable and loyal English gentleman who makes us all feel a little bit better about ourselves.

Aside from doing the earthy things in life, like eating real honey, holding wood clearing parties and appearing on BBC TV reality programmes, Dave's infectious enthusiasm has seen him win trophies galore and double up on the POTS award in recent years. With cavalier displays of batting to accompany his continuous haul of wickets, he was a natural fit for the role as T20 Captain. That bubbly zest for life has underscored a thus far more than successful reign.

Captain's comparison – Freddie Flintoff: pure box office, and a seemingly reluctant captain (given attendance). Does impressions, probably loves a sing-song, hits big, bowls quick, but is more loveable than Freddie.

Andrew Darley #098

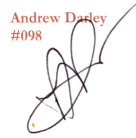

Enigmatic and gregariously upbeat, Andrew is one of those bubbly, larger-than-life characters who just begs your attention. Smashing stumps with 100mph bowling or hitting sixes into adjoining solar systems, it's all about IMPACT and SENSATIONALISM. Well, it is occasionally... when he isn't falling over his own stumps or tiptoeing precariously around the precipice of mental oblivion.

Generous and eternally exuberant about everything and anything, it's just a shame he isn't more enthusiastic about playing cricket for The MAD. Boasting one of the meanest bowling economies this club has ever known Andrew is often unplayable, due to being unavailable.

Captain's comparison – Andy Caddick; tall, rangy, and oft spellbinding with ball in hand. Can larrup a 6 or three as well. Enigma.

Ian Leggate #099

A true hedonist at heart, Gonzo's delightfully offbeat and eccentric humour has transcended many a MAD defeat. He is universally regarded as the essential tour accessory – colourfully unconventional, idiosyncratic and thriving in adversity. Thus it was with great sadness when the inevitable call of Northern Exposure came and Ian left these shores to start a family in Canada with his beloved Sandra (MAD Player #120).

Ian is still classed as a relatively, *kind-of* current player because he *did* indeed grace us with his presence during the season of 2015 (as well as netting in 2017), bringing along his new bairn and the Family Leggate to boot. It turned out bowling snowballs at Elks in the frozen wastelands didn't really translate to English summer cricket, facing as he did 11 balls for no runs and bowling one wicketless over. But hey, Gonzo's enthusiasm for the game and life in general remains unsullied.

Captain's comparison – Phil Tufnell; sensible strong chat about the game but talks nonsense about anything else. Capable of moments of pure magic.

David Emerson #105

Engaging, knowledgeable, flawed and talented in equal measure, Kiwi David joined the FFTMCC back in the late noughties, juggling permanent intoxication with a rash of ducks and a swathe of match winning bowling performances. The thing is, he was actually a batsman, he *always* was, but nobody ever asked him. The Club had a paucity of decent bowlers back in the day henceforth David *had* to be a bowler. Sorry about that ole boy.

On Tour to Pompey in 2011, Mr Emerson would smash 95 and secure back-to-back POTS awards before his body eventually, nay inevitably, collapsed under the strain. Of course, it was all Skipper Westmoreland's fault, flogging him like some unloved Muriwai Beach horse. Time is the greatest healer and in the intervening years, David has had remedial work with Thai masseurs, seen the Club psychiatrist and patched himself up with support tape. He's also decried bowling off any more than two paces and demanded to bat where he wants.

Captain's comparison – Talented Anglo-Kiwi with both bat and ball. Tattoos. Red Face. Probably going to be charged with affray.

James William Pearson #107

Astute, droll and eternally smug, James can mostly be found in a dreamlike sedentary state around the team's edges. When he isn't sick or comatose, which is a regular affliction, he's diligently surveying proceedings through those Daniel Vettori spectacles of his, eschewing his dulcet witticisms whilst popping a bottle of Belgium's finest; Leffe.

Since impressing his new team mates with 0 not out on debut, Corporal Pearson abseiled up The MAD batting order to win the prestigious 'Performance' Trophy in 2014 with an unbeaten ton against perennial rivals Isis CC. But to bracket James as purely a seasoned opener would to do a disservice to him, particularly when he's awake. He's also more than useful in the field and his many wickets almost always seem to go unnoticed.

Captain's comparison – Jacques Kallis; always up there in the stats sheets but no one really cares – which is their fault. Smug. "Batting above his average". Portly.

Chris Roberts #109

An amiable and genial giant, the congruent Mr Roberts is much akin to a loveable Great Dane – quietly and obediently performing whatever role he's given. Unperturbed by results or the tantrums and hysteria that surround him, this cordial and happy chappy just gets on with enjoying his sport with a smile on his face. Truth be

told, if we could bottle his DNA and sell it on to the Middle East we would.

In recent times, Bob has experienced a metamorphosis from hobbyist Kennel Club entrant to Crufts Best of Breed. He's always been useful in the field with that howitzer of an arm, but his bowling has come on exponentially – finally becoming that towering threat we always knew he could be. But what of his batting? Well he's had his MAD high score at #11 taken from him and he's actually quite bitter about that, especially as the guy who stole it was the same guy he destroyed at the Sambuca sponsored MAD Arm-Wrestling Championship in 2015.

Captain's comparison – Stuart Broad; when he gets it right, he really gets it right. Hit or miss with the bat. Easy to spot at an NFL tailgate.

Paddy Mellor #110

Gratifyingly charismatic and comedic, Paddy's engaging and warm humour has rubbed off on many of his team mates over the years. On signing up, he was immediately popular with the hardened pissheads at the Club, whereby there were many enticing layers to be discovered under that glitzy pink golf visor of his. Not least his ability pre-match to devour an entire roast dinner in absence of any cutlery.

Forever synonymous with organising *that* doomed Tour to f______ T______, Mr Mellor has at one point or another turned his hand to most things (other than running between the wickets with any urgency of course). His burgeoning MAD portfolio underscored with a limitless childlike enthusiasm boasts roles as Social Secretary, Tour Secretary, Partial Audley Ducks Fixture Secretary, Non-forthcoming Tour Coach Organising Secretary and Extortionate Fines Chairman.

Captain's comparison – Inzamam Ul Haq; block, block, block, whack. "Keeps" occasionally. Not keen on running.

Gareth Timms #112

Perceptive, enthusiastic and highly convivial, Gary was immediately recognised as having the necessary qualities for leadership, this despite his tender age of being less than forty. To the uninitiated, a casually sarcastic and insouciant character belied a notable IQ and rich appreciation of this sometimes-bewildering sport. He would make an instant splash as T20 Supremo following an undemocratic coup to remove Mr Hotson. The rapid ascent to seniority continued unabated, earning the respect of his minions to see his surname carved on The Captain's door. Time in office has thus far been kind, adhering to the ethos of The Club, he has nonetheless overseen successful MAD campaigns whilst navigating the team to their first ever cup final.

Despite renouncing freedom and getting hitched to the lovely Sara a few years ago, Gary's commitment to the Club has been unwavering. Making himself available for nearly every game, bar the Lemmings, he'll happily stand in the freezing wind and rain, cheerleading and directing his less than exultant team mates.

(Non) Captain's comparison – Jeremy Coney; not the best bowler, or the best batsman, but a leader of men. Even when those men don't particularly want to go anywhere.
(by Dave Emerson)

Lee Ainsworth #114

Cynical, downbeat and eternally grumpy, Lee finally made good on his word to leave his league frustrations behind to concentrate all his frustration on playing for The MAD in 2016. Technically gifted with bat and ball he plunders runs for fun when he isn't hitting full tosses straight to fielders. His cricketing nous is only bettered by his supremely gifted moaning; scarcely a minute passes without some barbed or disparaging remark concerning blinkered fielding positions or unnecessary slash ridiculous bowling changes.

Despite such a rich cricketing pedigree and instant formal standing, it is perhaps reassuring that chinks in his professional veneer are often exposed on Tour. One delights in recalling his alcoholic corpse being peeled off a hotel floor, poured into some whites, before being sent out to register a duck among the regal settings of Pylewell Park.

Captain's comparison - Jimmy Anderson; bowls with the correct hand, bats with the wrong one, and has a look that consistently suggests he feels his teammates aren't quite of his level.

Jonathan Newman-Robson #115

Pithy, competitive and exuding a malevolent sarcasm bordering on rude, the brickbat Mr Newman-Robson is famous as that guy who took the four-trick at Jordan Hill. Yep, that is FOUR WICKETS IN FOUR BALLS – and don't you forget it. He's also famous for succeeding in successfully transferring a nickname nobody really understands from a previous club to this.

Jon has never entertained T20 cricket. It's utter garbage in his eyes, for the avocado generation. Modern tosh for the cricket imposters who can't watch a game for five minutes without straying from their mobiles. Nah, our Jon is proper old school – a purist – he's all about grabbing the ball at the weekend, bowling his full stint at the start of the innings and then sloping off to whinge for the remainder. To be fair though, 2017's tour performance made us all glad of his aversion to the shorter short format.

Captain's comparison – Darren Gough; red face stocky (ish?) quick with a glint in the eye. Would like to think he could bat higher but has oft proved otherwise.

Mark Rundle #117

Cerebral and acidic, Mr Rundle brought a thoroughly intimidating nickname to The MAD at the start of the decade. On first impression, he seems unexpectedly mild-mannered, basking in an aura of calm and quiet understanding. Like all classically misaligned nutjobs, do not underestimate the calculated malevolence that lurks underneath. He'll soon compare you to female genitalia and drive a table fork through your eyeball during the tea interval if you do. A peripheral figure in the beginnings, Psycho has slowly become a recognised name on the team sheet, simply playing when and where he wants – and if you don't like it, well, see the previous sentence.

Mark has suffered in recent years from a myriad of aches and pains, not from fighting in the mosh pit you understand, but from carrying excess baggage around his waist and being less fit than he once was. Undeterred, he'll still saunter in to deliver that indescribable nothingness that bags him several wickets at a premium, bash a few runs down the order and spend the rest of his day pulling punches and riling anyone who hasn't heard his latest deplorable, bad taste jokes.

Captain's comparison – Rory Kleinveldt; the sort of guy you're irritated to get out to, or irritated by when he whacks you, as he really doesn't look like he should be able to play. Timber carrying nagger. NAGGER.

Russ Turner #122

Don't let Homer's gelastic, frivolous mannerisms fool you, because lurking behind that lovable exterior is a seasoned and accomplished sportsman. Every club or sporting franchise could do with someone like Mr R. P. Turner – a kindly gentleman of boundless wisdom, energy and enthusiasm with no small measure of self-depreciation. He brought a civilised air of cricketing pedigree to the ranks in 2012 and has been a dependable go-to to pick up the slack when no one else can be arsed.

A printer by trade, and a dead ringer for his alter-ego Mike Ashley of Sports Direct fame, his extensive customer portfolio allows him the luxury of the latest custom-built, personalised four wheeler. He is quite the talk on the pub circuit too, happily throwing his monies across the bar and never once baulking at an eating contest. A resolute and stoic top order batsman, Russ gets his head down and grafts when others are back in the hutch bemoaning their carefree ways.

Captain's comparison – Mike Gatting; gluttonous (in every way) top order bat often bamboozled by slower pie.

Johannes van den Grootschnyke Webster #123

Leftfield, sarcastic and sublimely eccentric, the socially joyous Mr Webster also has the longest name for anyone born outside of Sri Lanka. Since debuting half a decade ago, he's entertained all with his unpredictably zany character both on and off the field. Acutely clever and well-studied, The MAD's maverick Dutchman is a genius with the pen – detailing in absurd detail the highs and lows of a cricket match, whilst sometimes starring in the leading role.

Unpredictable with both bat and ball, it's probably as baffling to Jan as it is to anyone else trying to understand the rhyme or reason to his highs and lows. Is he a top order bat, middle order or useful pyrotechnic tailender? And just what does he do with the ball? Bowling mercurial leggies one game and then steaming in to remove keeper OAP Carter's teeth the next....

Captain's comparison – Imran Tahir; I've no idea what he does with the ball, with the bat, or in the field. He's bloody good fun though and does look like he could injure himself at any given moment.

Nick Hill #124

Another Nick, a younger Nick, and one who actually turns up to play some cricket, albeit of the T20 variety. Actually, it's not cricket that Nick plays, it is of course baseball, but he plays it *so* well that nobody really notices. Unless you care to look at his bat of course, which isn't a Grey Nicholls per se, but a long and cylindrical club with Budweiser emblazoned on it.

Another in a long line of chosen applicants from the Centrica Sporting Portfolio, Mr N. S. Hill brought an effervescent and youthful vigour to Team MAD back in 2012. Exuding a likeable charm and no little knowledge about, er... baseball, there is a buzz of excited anticipation every time Nick strides out to bat. There's no doubt he can hit a home run and there's no doubt baseball doesn't work in cricket – however, it's great fun watching Nick try disprove the latter theory.

Captains comparison – Lance Klusener; throws it hard, hits it harder, tries hard with ball in hand. Disappeared.

Cornelius Vermaak #141

Upbeat and jovially enthusiastic, Cornelius' debut for The MAD *really* was a baptism of fire. Answering a plea for players for a double weekender in June 2017, he found himself dropped behind alcoholic lines to fend off a touring Battisford team. He equipped himself well, showcasing a willingness to bowl as a total of 300 loomed, and a willingness to bat as if the target needed chasing in less than 10 overs. Actually, subsequent visits to the crease suggest that is how he plays anyway.

Due to Mr Vermaak's infancy in the team, it is hard to gauge the real him, other than he seems at odds with our country's view that there isn't any nice South Africans. So what do we know? He's definitely nice, maybe *too* nice. He lives in Abingdon, he mends houses, he has a bird and, erm… that's about it. We also have no verification (as yet) he didn't flee his homeland following a spate of serial killings in the Highveld of Mpumalanga.

Captain's comparison – Steve Harmison; can swing a bit, hit away and when he gets the bowling radar right, is most handy. Ruddy useless sense of direction though.

Chris Williams #144

The sequel to Bladerunner took less time in production than it took for Williams to finally join his mates and play for The MAD. A player of consummate talent with a batting style that is candy for the eye, it's way too early to ascertain whether his Wayfarer's fee was exorbitant or not. Early indications are positive however, with swift merchandising and a pleasing dedication having him rock up on Tour within his first few weeks.

Prudent and judicious, a mischievous grin belies that inner child that ingratiates his team mates. Whilst the passage of time can alter ones' wardrobe, Chris is happy in his Happy Monday's, forever waiting for Bez to join him and get their melons twisted on the sidelines. A man of intricate layers, his FBI shades hide those piercing dark eyes, and maybe that's the whole point – he's undercover – that'd explain a lot.

Captain's comparison – Jason Roy; plays all formats as if they're T20's. And why bloody not?!

THE DARK WEB

A History of the Far from the MCC website

Ian Howarth

AN encyclopaedic, humourous and at times irreverent MAD website, this unholy alliance of the good, the bad and the downright slanderous never even got a mention in the club's first book release '*Not At This Level*'. Not even a glossed sticker or page insert as an afterthought, so going one better, here is the affirmation of its existence on that World Wide Web type of thing….

www.farfromthemcc.co.uk

The exact date of the website's inception is hard to qualify, although it is thought to be around the mid-2000's. The concept was thrashed out in James Hoskins' oil and garbage stained kitchen at 9 Priors Forge, a three storey bachelor pad adjacent to Cutteslowe Park, north Oxford. Now sold and inhabited by humans from a different era, and no doubt of a more civilised inclination, the memories of Matt Bullock, Ian Howarth and Antony Mann propagating ideas whilst getting shitfaced into the night remain. Or do they? And was Adrian Fisher, Jake Hotson and lodgers Steve Dobner and Thornton Smith also present? And if they were, was this evening in question actually a poker session and in no way related to cricket or creativity? What is certain is that unlike the often discussed ice-cream van that doubled as a mobile scorebox, the website *did* eventually come into fruition.

In its infancy, it was a basic fixtures and results template sat on a free hosting domain with a shoddy type font and gaudy background. From there it outgrew its tiny imprint on James' prehistoric laptop to find itself eventually hosted by 50Webs, a company purportedly based in the UK, but as readily could be located in someone's bedroom in the Ukraine. Either way, with the club having overpaid for the domain name and six millennia's of hosting it, the site should hopefully still be in existence long after we're all dead. Much like this book you are holding now, which if the club's committee has done its job properly, should also reside in the Bodleian Library, gathering dust and long forgotten with its own ISBN.

Over the past decade, the website has grown exponentially into a lauded compendium of everything from Jude the Obscure's halcyon days to the Far from the MCC of the present. A grandiose labour of love, its two and half gigabyte mass is now maintained under the studios rigours of Mr Howarth, self-appointed editor and chief and erstwhile OCD sufferer. Though if you were to ask David Emerson, he would counter that final descriptive, telling you that other than the booze, Ian has no real afflictions and that he is simply an obsessive with a propensity for being overly tidy.

The chore and champion of The MAD website is the '*Reports & Scorecards*' section, a detailed repository charting *every* single one of the club's four hundred and forty four

Three geniuses discover a laptop in the early 21st century

matches to date, all the way back to May 24, 1998 when The Jude were comprehensively beaten by Research Machines at… coincidentally, Cutteslowe Park. Matt Bullock's staggeringly comprehensive collection of scorecards are complemented almost a year later by Antony Mann's first ever journalistic work†, which details the match against Isis CC in which the opposition didn't actually lose, going under the expansive title '*Upset Number Three for Jude – Pundits Under Attack*'. Ant's whimsical and pithy observations amused the team for close to a decade, and his skilful undertakings have acted as inspiration for others long after he sadly departed. Written mostly under a variety of pseudonyms, reportage from *others* can be categorised as ranging from the good, the bad and the downright libellous, but whatever their hand, they retain indelible moments of times chiefly unremembered. Mr A. G. Mann was also the originator of *Inspectorates* and *Player Tour Ratings*, oblique and jocular observations and side-stories that continue today.

The "adult" friendly match reports are richly imbued with plenty of photographic work these days, the quality of which has steadily improved with each passing year. The educated, startlingly defined long lens images of today are lightyears away from their grainy, camera phone generated relatives. Back then, Vodafone was struggling under the financial burden of James Hoskins' distribution of mobiles to his team mates. A maverick of his times, JMO would stand as umpire holding a Nokia in front of his chest clicking away as the distracted batsman was then bowled. Now considered bad form, this practice is mostly outlawed by the club, notably after a Steve Dobner duck preceded a threat to the umpire's (team mate's) general welfare.

Despite dissenting voices, *Match Fines* have also been an integral part of MAD culture over the years, publicised in detail these amusing, outrageous and often cruel taxes have often supplemented the match reports. A draconian kangaroo court of sorts, the

† *Back in the sepia toned days before the club understood what the internet was, Ant's original match reports were printed on a small laserjet and distributed amongst the team at the following game. Of impressive literary hand, they nonetheless had more than one use, particularly if the groundsman had failed to stock the toilets sufficiently.*

popularity of these post-match sessions has seen a dip in popularity in recent years, particularly under the *extreme* gavelling of judge and juror, Mr P. A. S. Mellor. Under his merciless vindictive reign, Paddy's most infamous haul came at Happisburgh on the tour to Norfolk in 2012, where he turned on his team mates to the tune of a staggering *£126.50*. This goldmine for The MAD treasury department included Mike Reeves' not insubstantial taxes of £19.75, with a classic pre-game levy for "*Leading Dave Shorten off a cliff whilst admiring a lighthouse.*"

An excellent method to bring the more raucous and mulish members of the team into line, fines nonetheless ended up persecuting the quieter and more affable members. Sat there minding his own with a quiet pint, Tall Bob would watch dejectedly as the same old fine was trotted out after every game: *Playing cricket with his head in the clouds.*

Being dismissed in cricket is a dispiriting and generally sombre affair, but with the advent of MAD technology, the club chose to celebrate these fleeting moments of ineptitude with the grand unveiling of the '*Exhibition of Batting Incompetence*' (or EBI section of the website). Charting over a decade of these timber rattling swipes at thin air, this photographic showcase by luminaires Hoskins, Howarth, Bullock and Hotson, has sought to capture these shambolic, split-second moments of dross in all their glory. Just as you should champion those who succeed, this English pub team with *no* pub, champions those who would fail, embracing inadequacy to the delight and amusement of all. It's why Sunday cricket exists, lest we forget not to take ourselves so bloody seriously. On display overleaf are a select portfolio of some of the more prodigious exhibits, entrance of course is free.

Every sports club has its characters, some legendary, some less so, regardless of whatever their charms, criminal pastimes, political standing or choice of beer, they are the heartbeat without which these enterprises wither and die. Celebrating a grand total of one hundred and forty five human beings to play for The MAD since its inception, the '*Player*' section of the website categorises these individuals into those considered *Current* and those *Non-Current*, with anyone not deemed worth a write-up to be found included in an incremental *Historical List* (founding member Edmund Neil Lester was player #1, who opened the batting in match #1 and needless to say was adjudged LBW). Again, the exact date of the first player profiling is unknown, although one suspects these droll, disparaging yet positive little send-ups were originally crafted in that same squalid kitchen at Prior's Forge. Facetious and uncensored, they've morphed over the years into becoming furtherly facetious, but now tarted up with longer words researched from an online thesaurus and razor sharp portrait and action shots. They also carry the additional weight and illumination of Matt's wicked nous with numbers.

One thing that hasn't changed is many cases are the nicknames, some stick and some don't, and I can't give you an explanation, other than some of these *names* just seem to resonate more than others. *Spam* will always be *Spam* on account of the amount of shit he sends via email, *Moo* will *always* be *Moo* despite Martin Westmoreland having an

EBI exhibit I: Martin Westmoreland, at Aston Tirrold, 2011

EBI exhibit II: James Pearson, versus Cholsey at Brasenose, 2011

EBI exhibit III: David Emerson, at Enstone, 2013

EBI exhibit IV: Mike Reeves, at Garsington, 2013

EBI exhibit V: Ian Howarth, at Appleton, 2014

EBI exhibit VI: Dave Shorten, versus The Bodleian at Brasenose, 2015

EBI exhibit VII: Gary Timms, at Marlborough School, 2015

EBI exhibit VIII: Andy Darley, at Freeland, 2017

assortment of names on his back over the years. You can call him what you want, most do, but he's still *Moo* and he still moo's the ball to cow corner. Conversely, *Lego* is *Hang Time* who is actually Dave Shorten, a builder by trade who floats in the air before delivery, but a recent dietary disclosure may well see a new nickname stick. '*Gruel*', anyone? Or maybe *Oliver* (Twist)? Seriously, does anyone else in the right mind actually eat that impoverished Victorian muck anymore…?

Originally new players were allocated a name by the club, now it seems they either transfer an existing one (*Psycho* – Mark Rundle former OU Offices, *Salad* – Jon Newman former Wayfarers) or it simply comes into being because of all the incessant moaning done (*Chunter* – Lee Ainsworth). They're all good fun, slowly peeling away from discoloured shirts for all to see, with James Pearson's maybe the funniest, *Fattori* being a cruel comparison with a fictionally fat Daniel Vettori (New Zealand cricketer). He sportingly agreed to have the number 3.14 printed on his shirt too… equivalent of pi (geddit?)

Increasingly aware of a raft of MAD memorabilia that maybe lost during his journey back down under, Antony Mann hatched the idea of a '*Museum*' section of the website. The doors of which opened in the mid-noughties with many fascinating (or not) artefacts on display, ranging from camouflaged tour radios, broken bats, toilet seat

Above:The curator of the now deceased museum: Ant Mann
Right: Tall Bob and Tall Bob, otherwise known as George and Lennie, otherwise known as....

medallions and an abusive sticker which appeared on the back of Howarth's bat once upon a time, later to be rediscovered in Ant's teenage son's kitbag (donated by Spam).

Although amusing, the doors of the museum would close in 2014, with its entire collection being swallowed up by the all-encompassing MAD '*Glossary*'. This seismic multi-page area of the website was first suggested back in 2006, when Mike Reeves joined the club from a shit pub team worse than our own, admitting he hadn't got a ruddy clue what most people were going on about. His idea found support, and thus it was this graffiti daubed toilet door became your *go to place* for all your *0-9* and *A-Z* MAD references, lingo, tales and folklore. Embellished with a billion or so images, quotes and short descriptions, this comic book extravaganza is many people's favourite page, ridiculing and polarising all that is great and not so great about this club.

Cricket is after all a statisticians' dream, henceforth where would the website be without a monumental vault of numbers, aggregates and '*Records*'? And how can the club ever repay the debt of gratitude owed to chairman Bullock's tireless work over so many winter months? Dutifully compiling details of nearly every single ball bowled into one ginormous, bewildering Excel database spanning two decades, it spits out facts and figures you wouldn't even imagine, records you never thought were possible, and of course the painful end of season averages where we mostly wonder where it all went wrong. Matt's stats will no doubt find new admiration at the end of this book and in particular extracts from the laudable *Duck* section, the finest depot of bungled batting anywhere on the planet. Without this dizzying armada of numbers, many of us would have little to moan and argue about, and without that, what really is the point of us playing anymore (in case you were left wondering)?

Of course any website worth its stripes will inevitably become the target of hackers over time, and Mr Howarth was alerted in the late 2000's to the front header page containing a well-endowed lady chowing down on a sizeable manhood. On removal of said image and other offensive material, Ian was subsequently inundated by complaints from his team mates. *That* infamous photograph was not reposted.

As we go to press, or to Mr Turner's wonderful, market leading Fineprint company (shameless plug), the website's counters and trackers argue we've been hit in excess of 32,518 times, and that behind the United Kingdom, the United States and Brazil are marginally fixated in our own shortcomings as much as the curious holder of this book. I also note that recent visitors originate from Bologna and Albufeira, which may account for Nick Hill seeking new employment in Italy and me sat on my arse in the Algarve typing out this twaddle. Amusingly, I furtherly note that as far as using internet search engines go, "*the*" is the fourth most active keyword in discovering the *Far from the MCC*.

The. End of this chapter. ■

FANTASY CRICKET

A Brief History

James Hoskins

I STILL remember the time clearly when MAD Fantasy Cricket was conceived – travelling down the M40 (or were we on the M25 by then?), four (or was it five?) MADsters on an out of season social in late 2005 (or was it early 2006?) – we were definitely in Moo's car (I think) and very definitely on our way to see Stevie D (although I can't remember why), so yes, crystal clear memories indeed.

I think we were talking about Fantasy Football and I think I was probably commenting on how shit it was that we all spent hours poring over Fantasy Football Costs to enter a team into a National Newspaper for a fiver only to find five weeks later that we were in 141,323rd position out of 143,158 entrants, with little or no idea of who we had picked in the first place and very little interest remaining in the whole thing.

How much more fun it would be if we could play Fantasy *Cricket* we all thought….and hang on, what if we did it with our OWN team? By the time we had rolled up in Stevenage the seed had been set, a basic format drawn out and MAD Fantasy Cricket was alive. With a genuine interest in the mathematical challenges (of creating a costing algorithm to ensure it would not be an easy task to select a team you really wanted without spending all available resources) I enthusiastically volunteered to run the competition for the following season... just to see how it went….

It is indeed quite a challenge to ensure all of the players are priced in such a way so their cost reflects potential point scoring ability over the forthcoming season and no doubt readers are wondering the exact ins-and-outs of the algorithm that produces the costings. But I couldn't possibly reveal that (since it is not an exact science). Suffice to say it is a subtle mix of previous form (over as long as the player has been playing), net rumours and head sizes. I've always thought that an indication of getting the pricing policy right is the variance in teams selected – and over the years there have only ever been a handful of duplicate teams. Although as Jake once pointed out to me, that might have something to do with the fact that there are 593,775 possible ways of selecting 6 players out of 30!

Now, due to a fatal backup failure at the end of the 2010 season (and it wasn't a MAC in those days) original MAD Fantasy records have sadly been lost in the ether, but I seem to remember that we had about ten teams entering that first year for a meagre £25 first prize. Year on year the popularity and intrigue of the competition has seen the number of entries soar to over 50, with the most recent First prize award of £135! If current trends continue as shown by the graph over the page we should hit 100 entries by the year 2028!

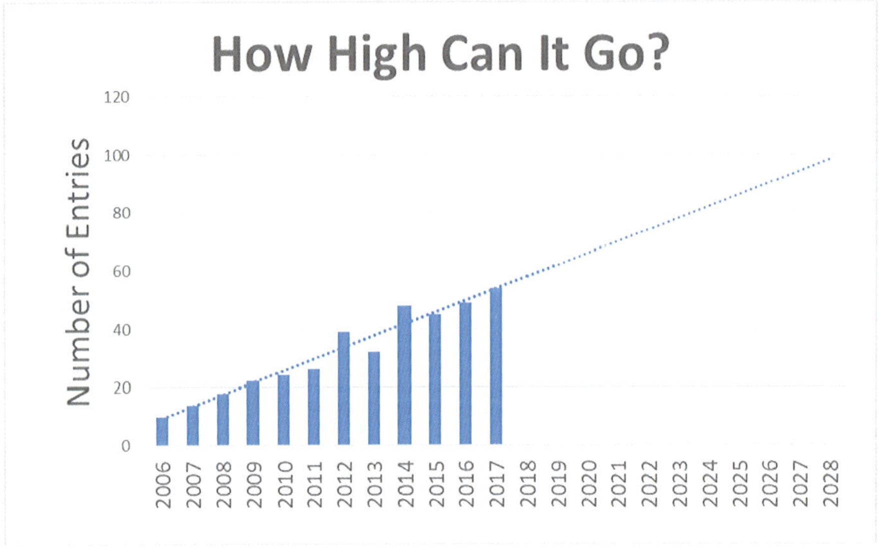

Over the years the rules have been tinkered and tailored. Most rule changes have stayed – I think the only rule change that was reversed was that of 'substitutions' – an idea to keep your interest as a Team Manager should one of your players become injured or have a baby mid-season. I have no idea why I thought that one would be possible to administer and substitutions were quickly replaced by 'Jokers' as a way for lower rank teams to boost their way up the table. Jokers remain as a popular feature and now include not only Sunday game Joker play, but also T20 Jokers and the horrendously complicated (if your name is Darley) 'Tour' Jokers.

Rundle (left) amusing some idiot with some deeply offensive joke

For history's sake here *are* the rules:

Select six players for your MAD Fantasy Cricket Team that cost a total of no more than 100 points. Not forgetting to name your team something obscure (see Mark Rundle), insulting (see Mark Rundle), deeply offensive (see Mark Rundle), or bizarre (erm... see Mark Rundle).

Points are awarded to players in your team thus:

Runs	1	T20 Match Economy <5	25
Sunday Match 50s	25	Hat-tricks	50
Sunday Match 100s	50	Stumping	15
T20 Match 30s	25	Zero Byes Bonus	10
T20 Match 50s	50	Low Byes Bonus (up to 5)	5
Ducks	-10	Catch	10
Wickets	15	Direct Run Out	10
Sunday Match 4-for	25	Shared Run Out	5
Sunday Match 5-for	50	Drops	-5
T20 Match 3-for	25	Buffet	-5
T20 Match 4-for	50	>25 Batting Average over season	50
Sunday Match Economy <3	25	<15 Bowling Average over season	50

A Joker can be played on your team for one Sunday game and one T20 during the season for which your Team's points will be trebled and a Joker can be played on any touring player in your Team for which that Player's points scored on tour will be trebled.

Rule changes as expected are directly proportional to the number of queries I get about the rules, but in the case of a certain Mr A. Darley, rule changes particularly surrounding Jokers are exponentially proportional to the number of queries I get as shown by the graph over the page.

Basic rules indeed, but it's remarkable how much confusion this can cause in MAD ranks – such as the absolute total misunderstanding of the whole point of the game after a certain Mr D. Edwards entered a team costing 142 points which consisted of the six most expensive players. I seem to remember an email chain ensued:

Dan: "Well I want those six because they are the best."
Me: "But you can't afford them."
Dan: "Who can I afford then?"
Me: "Six players that cost no more than 100."

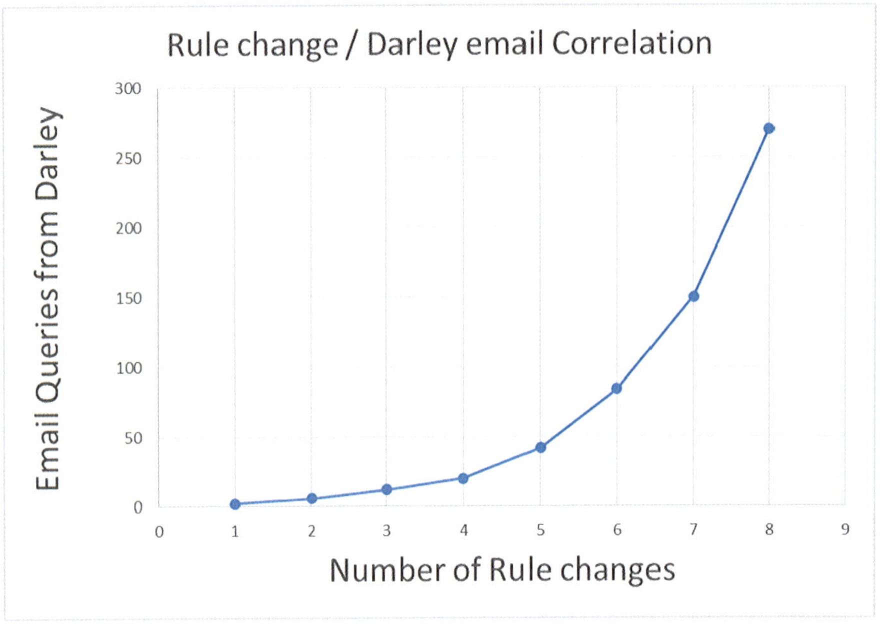

Dan: "So who can I swap out of my team?"
Me: "For example you can swap Howarth out for Dobner and it will save you ten points."
Dan: "I'll do that then."
Me: "OK, so now your team costs 132 points."
Dan: "So who else can I drop?"
Me: "You could have the bottom six players."
Dan: "But half of them don't even play."

…and so it went on….

It has to be said I am not without fault during the scoring of the Fantasy Points following a match. No matter how carefully I pore over the scorecard I often seem to forget to account for a catch; or an Economy Bonus; or some clever algorithm I have put into my spreadsheet fails to account for a Duck; or a typo in a player's name means they aren't credited for their points… but it's usually within about three minutes of sending out the summary mail that I will get a flurry of emails from the player I forgot the catch/bonus for; the Managers who have that player in their teams and most consistently of all – a certain Mr G. Timms who I am sure has a Fantasy Cricket Spreadsheet all of his own installed permanently in his Cerebrum which updates ball by ball as the Match unfolds. I am eternally grateful to all these corrections as it keeps us all honest and above all, means that people are actually paying attention – so that must be a good sign.

I am proud of the fact that Fantasy Cricket continues to entertain and has become an integral part of MAD ethos. Discussion ensues pre-match around whether or not to play Jokers and often in the field you can hear that extra groan from a Fantasy Manager when one of their Players drops a catch. Post-match comes the accusations of dropped Fantasy points or handshakes for good Fantasy performances.

So, since we are all gluttons for statistics – here are a few MAD Fantasy stats for our amusement:

Record of Winners:

Manager	Year
L. G. Ainsworth	2017
J. W. Pearson	2016
C. D. Roberts	2015
D. Shorten	2014
R. P. Turner	2013
J. W. Pearson	2012
J. W. Pearson	2011
T. P. W. Smith	2010
J. D. Hoskins	2009
J. D. Hoskins	2008
M. K. Reeves	2007
G. S. Littlechild	2006

Highest Fantasy Points scored by a single player in a Match: 211 J. Newman-Robson (vs OUP 2013)

Highest Total Team Fantasy Point Score in a Season: 5,128 C. D. Roberts (Cheese and Pineapple)

Number of cells in the 2017 Fantasy spreadsheet: 123,475 (no wonder I make so many mistakes!) ■

RECORDS AND STATISTICS

Matt Bullock

QUITE how I got the job of club statistician has never been properly established, but probably stems from the fact that I made my debut in match number 4 in 1998 so have witnessed many of the games and have met most of the people who have represented our club over the years. Back in the day at Jude the Obscure, we had the use of a noticeboard in the pub and scorecards and averages were the obvious thing to display upon it, if just to prove to the customers that we did exist, and we did actually play cricket. The first scorebook was lost somewhere in Swindon in 2000, so thankfully some record of these early games survived, even if the details are a bit sketchy.

A plethora of statistics and records is provided on our website so there was little point reproducing it here, even if there was space. Below is a summary of every season, and over the following five pages you will find the career batting, bowling and fielding records of all 145 players who have turned out for the club.

Year	Club Captain	M	W	D	T	L	Ab	Runs	HS	0	50	100	Wkts	Best	5wi	ct	st	ro
1998	E.N. Lester	8	2			6		652	86	16	3		36	5-24	1	22	2	
1999	E.N. Lester	13	4			7	2	1169	68	27	3		74	6-23	2	31		3
2000	E.N. Lester	17	4			13		1399	73	29	3		103	5-9	1	38	8	2
2001	L. Phillips	13	4			9		1511	97 *	16	8		81	5-28	1	30	4	2
2002	M. Bullock	11	2			9		830	58	21	1		69	4-17		26		
2003	J.D. Hoskins	20	7			13		2348	97	31	7		134	4-7		63	3	5
2004	J.D. Hoskins	20	9			11		2420	95	41	9		140	5-15	2	66	4	7
2005	J.D. Hoskins	16	7			8	1	1914	99	14	11		118	7-5	1	49		8
2006	I. Howarth	15	9			6		2183	117 *	14	7	4	107	4-9		41	5	7
2007	I. Howarth	17	11			6		2136	112	29	8	1	137	4-9		56	6	2
2008	I. Howarth	16	7	1		6	2	1544	82	19	4		106	4-16		60		11
2009	M.T. Westmoreland	25	10	2	1	11	1	3014	101 *	33	14	1	161	5-5	4	84	1	9
2010	M.T. Westmoreland	28	13		1	13	1	3601	102	31	12	1	200	4-12		79	4	8
2011	M.T. Westmoreland	35	9			26		4034	109 *	72	14	1	207	5-20	4	73	7	28
2012	M.T. Westmoreland	24	7		1	16		2667	89	35	4		125	4-26		50	3	23
2013	M.T. Westmoreland	34	11			22	1	3392	77	54	6		212	5-10	1	97	3	20
2014	I. Howarth	31	10			20	1	3267	113 *	38	5	2	176	5-12	1	79	1	30
2015	G.J. Timms	33	20		2	11		4013	73	40	7		206	4-15		88	6	23
2016	G.J. Timms	31	19			11	1	3660	87	31	14		194	4-22		81	7	17
2017	G.J. Timms	37	13			22	2	4172	88	48	10		207	4-19		98	8	34
	TOTAL	444	178	3	5	246	12	49926	117 *	639	150	10	2793	7-5	18	1211	72	239

Career Records - Batting

Note that prior to 2000 the number of balls faced was not recorded, hence the majority of players from the early years have no strike rate recorded.

	Career Records	Seasons	M	I	NO	R	HS	AVE	BF	SR	0	50	100
001	Edmund Lester	1998-2004	73	68	9	607	33 *	10.29		-	9		
002	Martin Hurley	1998-2000	13	13	0	106	25	8.15		-	3		
003	Chris Legg	1998-2000	14	14	2	200	49	16.67		-	1		
004	Fred Townsend	1998-1999	12	10	1	23	4	2.56		-	1		
005	Ben Parkinson	1998	1	1	0	2	2	2.00		-			
006	Nick Banks	1998	2	2	0	4	4	2.00		-	1		
007	Patrick O'Sullevan	1998	1	1	0	1	1	1.00		-			
008	Michael Brandon	1998	2	1	0	0	0	0.00		-	1		
009	Jon Moore	1998-1999	7	5	1	2	2	0.50		-	2		
010	James Blann	1998-1999	9	9	0	96	32	10.67		-	2		
011	Nash Pal	1998	1	1	0	7	7	7.00		-			
012	Richard Blann	1998-1999	3	2	1	18	11 *	18.00		-			
013	Sam Pollard	1998-2001	10	6	2	19	9 *	4.75		-	2		
014	James Townsend	1998-1999	5	3	0	3	2	1.00		-	2		
015	Simon Brandon	1998	5	5	0	210	86	42.00		-		2	
016	Antony Mann	1998-2012	137	104	34	964	58	13.77		-	10	1	
017	James A Moore	1998-1999	5	4	1	30	17 *	10.00		-	3		
018	Matt Bullock	1998-2017	223	190	25	1585	41 *	9.61		-	31		
019	Howard Jones	1998-2004	34	35	5	874	78 *	29.13		-	5	8	
020	Kevin	1998	1	1	0	1	1	1.00		-			
021	Noel Reilly	1998-2000	3	3	0	3	3	1.00		-	2		
022	Adrian Deans	1998	1	1	0	1	1	1.00		-			
023	Lee Davie	1998-2005	14	13	3	557	97 *	55.70		-		5	
024	Leo Beletsky	1999	1	1	0	7	7	7.00		-			
025	Mike Thorburn	1999-2001	18	16	0	169	44	10.56		-	4		
026	Robert Phillips	1999	3	3	0	8	8	2.67		-	2		
027	James Hoskins	1999-2017	302	226	48	1496	50	8.40		-	42	1	
028	Stuart Redfern	1999	1	1	0	32	32	32.00		-			
029	Matthew Lloyd	1999	1	1	0	0	0	0.00		-	1		
030	Simon Dickens	1999	2	2	2	30	17 *	-		-			
031	Philip Holt	1999-2000	3	2	0	3	2	1.50	21	14.29			
032	Clare Norris	1999-2000	15	13	3	28	9	2.80		-	5		
033	Michael O'Leary	1999	2	3	0	3	3	1.00		-	2		
034	Gus Da Cenha	1999	1	1	0	1	1	1.00		-			
035	Tony Mander	1999-2010	68	62	12	318	34	6.36		-	17		
036	Ben Mander	1999-2012	68	60	14	409	29	8.89		-	11		
037	Jess Ball	1999	1	1	0	1	1	1.00		-			
038	James Dale	1999	1	1	0	0	0	0.00		-	1		
039	Paul Grant	2000	6	6	0	18	8	3.00		-	1		
040	Lorcan Kennan	2000	5	5	1	22	7 *	5.50		-			
041	James Yarwood	2000	1	1	0	10	10	10.00		-			
042	Greg Le Tocq	2000	12	9	2	41	21 *	5.86		-	3		
043	Paul Drake	2000-2002	12	11	1	73	22	7.30		-	1		
044	Andrew Morley	2000-2010	51	41	5	91	27	2.53		-	18		
045	Leo Phillips	2000-2002	16	15	1	213	44 *	15.21		-	2		
046	Adrian Fisher	2000-2011	48	44	7	502	44	13.57		-	4		
047	Jake Hotson	2000-2017	265	209	39	1016	26	5.98		-	43		
048	Nick Watney	2000	3	3	1	33	21 *	16.50	50	66.00			
049	Lloyd Mike	2000	1	1	1	20	20 *	-	24	83.33			
050	Richard Hadfield	2000-2017	48	47	12	1037	88	29.63	1428	72.62	3	3	
051	Steve Ray	2000	1	1	0	4	4	4.00	6	66.67			
052	Steve Merivale	2000	1	1	0	2	2	2.00	9	22.22			
053	Kate Atkinson	2000	1	1	0	0	0	0.00	5	0.00	1		
054	James Smith	2000	1	1	1	4	4 *	-	8	50.00			
055	Steven Walker	2000-2002	4	4	0	14	10	3.50	57	24.56	1		

	Career Records	Seasons	M	I	NO	R	HS	AVE	BF	SR	0	50	100
056	Steve Dobner	2001-2017	184	170	26	2181	84	15.15	3887	56.11	23	5	
057	Thornton Smith	2001-2017	232	206	34	1753	65	10.19	2653	66.08	35	3	
058	Mike Rogers	2001	1	1	0	1	1	1.00	8	12.50			
059	James Mander	2001	6	6	1	23	14	4.60	51	45.10	2		
060	Grant Smart	2001	1	1	0	24	24	24.00	21	114.29			
061	Atul	2001	1	1	0	9	9	9.00	11	81.82			
062	John Greany	2001	1	1	0	70	70	70.00	71	98.59		1	
063	Matt Baker	2001	1	1	0	10	10	10.00	12	83.33			
064	Niraj	2001	1	1	0	0	0	0.00	5	0.00	1		
065	Dylan Jones	2002-2004	21	20	4	67	14	4.19	145	46.21	7		
066	Jay	2002	1	1	0	12	12	12.00	26	46.15			
067	Shaki	2002	1	1	0	0	0	0.00	2	0.00	1		
068	Ian Harwood	2002	2	2	0	0	0	0.00	5	0.00	2		
069	Nigel Sawyer	2002	1	1	1	2	2 *	-	2	100.00			
070	David Grundy	2002	1	1	0	1	1	1.00	6	16.67			
071	Nick Hebbes	2003-2017	107	95	14	1456	62	17.98	2675	54.43	11	4	
072	Martin Westmoreland	2003-2017	258	239	36	3954	109 *	19.48	5544	71.32	22	12	2
073	Steve Hebbes	2003-2008	27	22	9	161	33	12.38	264	60.98	5		
074	John Harris	2003-2008	28	21	5	260	48	16.25	504	51.59	2		
075	Graham Bridges	2003-2004	16	16	1	63	16 *	4.20	166	37.95	4		
076	Paul Henley	2003	1	1	0	1	1	1.00	3	33.33			
077	Ian Howarth	2003-2017	305	274	46	7175	112	31.47	8094	88.65	22	45	2
078	Shoaib Ahmed	2003	1	1	1	3	3 *	-	1	300.00			
079	Sudharkar Selveraj	2003	1	0				-		-			
080	Justin Jackman	2003	1	2	0	10	6	5.00	12	83.33			
081	Neil Howarth	2003	1	1	0	14	14	14.00	8	175.00			
082	Marco	2003	1	1	0	0	0	0.00	1	0.00	1		
083	Michael Horton	2003	1	1	0	2	2	2.00	15	13.33			
084	Paul Williams	2004	1	1	0	18	18	18.00	26	69.23			
085	Michael Clarke	2004-2009	24	18	1	203	61	11.94	276	73.55	3	1	
086	Dan Edwards	2004-2012	123	119	26	3158	103 *	33.96	5536	57.04	5	15	2
087	Gary Littlechild	2005-2010	30	28	5	920	117 *	40.00	1029	89.41	1	6	1
088	Victoria Stone	2005	1	1	0	0	0	0.00	5	0.00	1		
089	Geoff Carter	2005-2017	108	91	9	706	39	8.61	1772	39.84	17		
090	Richard Kemp-Harper	2005	1	1	1	14	14 *	-	15	93.33			
091	Steven Arnold	2005	1	0				-		-			
092	Andy Cavanagh	2006	10	8	1	48	16	6.86	104	46.15	2		
093	Mike Reeves	2006-2017	226	188	51	2565	85	18.72	3259	78.71	20	5	
094	Steve Parkinson	2006-2016	27	23	5	292	39	16.22	426	68.54	3		
095	Adrian Small	2006-2008	20	9	4	34	10	6.80	69	49.28	2		
096	Dave Shorten	2006-2017	160	140	30	2022	103 *	18.38	2132	94.84	18	2	1
097	Petr Benisek	2007	2	1	0	2	2	2.00	3	66.67			
098	Andrew Darley	2008-2017	46	37	3	326	52	9.59	407	80.10	8	1	
099	Ian Leggate	2008-2015	72	62	9	211	31 *	3.98	578	36.51	23		
100	Huw Leggate	2008	1	1	0	17	17	17.00	22	77.27			
101	Jenner Collins	2008-2011	4	4	0	209	102	52.25	185	112.97		1	1
102	JP Collins	2008-2009	15	12	5	118	27	16.86	121	97.52	1		
103	Andy Washington	2008	1	1	0	0	0	0.00	8	0.00	1		
104	Alex Washington	2008	1	1	0	1	1	1.00	11	9.09			
105	Dave Emerson	2009-2017	168	141	20	1848	95	15.27	1935	95.50	20	2	
106	Brad Harsant	2009	2	2	0	4	4	2.00	9	44.44	1		
107	James Pearson	2010-2017	147	134	28	2185	113 *	20.61	3421	63.87	16	11	1
108	Ross Maher	2010	1	1	0	0	0	0.00	1	0.00	1		
109	Chris Roberts	2010-2017	177	121	34	433	19	4.98	658	65.81	27		
110	Paddy Mellor	2010-2017	61	59	2	452	41	7.93	850	53.18	10		
111	Jack Cox	2010	1	1	0	0	0	0.00	6	0.00	1		
112	Gareth Timms	2010-2017	159	116	30	714	45	8.30	1013	70.48	27		
113	Ted Jordan	2010	1	1	1	9	9 *	-	4	225.00			
114	Lee Ainsworth	2011-2017	63	55	13	1569	83	37.36	2071	75.76	2	11	
115	Jon Newman-Robson	2011-2017	57	37	10	204	24	7.56	328	62.20	5		

	Career Records	Seasons	M	I	NO	R	HS	AVE	BF	SR	0	50	100
116	Rob Eaglestone	2011-2012	7	6	0	11	5	1.83	25	44.00	3		
117	Mark Rundle	2011-2017	71	45	15	220	31 *	7.33	491	44.81	10		
118	Ralph Smith	2011	1	1	0	34	34	34.00	37	91.89			
119	Rob Arkell	2011	1	0				-		-			
120	Sandra Steinhauer	2011	1	1	0	0	0	0.00	9	0.00	1		
121	James Shaw	2011	1	1	0	11	11	11.00	13	84.62			
122	Russell Turner	2012-2017	130	125	21	2128	63	20.46	3590	59.28	9	4	
123	Jan Webster	2012-2017	36	29	7	213	30	9.68	386	55.18	7		
124	Nick Hill	2012-2017	38	32	3	279	31 *	9.62	286	97.55	5		
125	John Nash	2012	1	1	0	1	1	1.00	7	14.29			
126	Jamie Whiting	2012	1	1	0	19	19	19.00	15	126.67			
127	Adam Ward	2013	10	9	0	149	34	16.56	268	55.60	1		
128	Hugo Scott	2013	4	3	0	37	19	12.33	89	41.57	1		
129	Steve Lawrence	2013	1	0				-		-			
130	Rahman Aliza	2013	2	1	0	32	32	32.00	33	96.97			
131	Stuart Ackland	2013	2	0				-		-			
132	Dan Emerson	2013-2015	3	2	0	0	0	0.00	13	0.00	2		
133	Matt Reading	2014-2016	14	12	5	52	18 *	7.43	81	64.20	4		
134	Quintin Sanders	2014-2015	1	1	0	5	5	5.00	19	26.32			
135	Mark Shelley	2014-2015	2	2	1	7	7 *	7.00	16	43.75	1		
136	Sami Mughal	2016	2	0				-		-			
137	Graham Wilson	2016	1	0				-		-			
138	Nick Parnell-Smith	2016	1	1	1	0	0 *	-	12	0			
139	Dave Barlow	2017	1	1	1	13	13 *	-	12	108.333			
140	Polly Moon	2017	1	1	1	1	1 *	-	16	6.25			
141	Cornelius Vermaak	2017	7	5	0	31	18	6.20	38	81.58	2		
142	Srinivasan Janarthanan	2017	1	1	0	3	3	3.00	9	33.33			
143	Daniel Shaw	2017	1	1	0	9	9	9.00	10	90.00			
144	Chris Williams	2017	12	10	2	217	43 *	27.13	209	103.83			
145	Simon Coates	2017	1	1	1	2	2 *	-	31	6.45			

Career Records - Bowling & Fielding

	Career Records	Seasons	M	O	M	R	W	Best	Ave	Econ	SR	5wi	ct	st	ro	tot
001	Edmund Lester	1998-2004	73	192 . 4	6	1006	35	3-11	28.74	5.22	33.03		16			16
002	Martin Hurley	1998-2000	13						-	-	-				1	1
003	Chris Legg	1998-2000	14	67	2	365	16	3-16	22.81	5.45	25.13		2			2
004	Fred Townsend	1998-1999	12	60	1	361	10	5-24	36.10	6.02	36.00	1	7			7
005	Ben Parkinson	1998	1	1	0	13	0	0-13	-	13.00	-					0
006	Nick Banks	1998	2						-	-	-		1			1
007	Patrick O'Sullevan	1998	1						-	-	-					0
008	Michael Brandon	1998	2	4	0	26	0	0-26	-	6.50	-					0
009	Jon Moore	1998-1999	7	25	1	132	6	2-20	22.00	5.28	25.00		1			1
010	James Blann	1998-1999	9	36	3	210	7	2-23	30.00	5.83	30.86		6			6
011	Nash Pal	1998	1	2	0	26	0	0-26	-	13.00	-		1			1
012	Richard Blann	1998-1999	3	7 . 2	0	77	2	2-62	38.50	10.50	22.00					0
013	Sam Pollard	1998-2001	10	17	0	97	3	2-17	32.33	5.71	34.00		3			3
014	James Townsend	1998-1999	5	3	1	6	1	1-6	6.00	2.00	18.00		2			2
015	Simon Brandon	1998	5	23 . 3	0	106	5	3-6	21.20	4.51	28.20		1			1
016	Antony Mann	1998-2012	137	820 . 2	152	2471	191	5-25	12.94	3.01	25.77	1	65		4	69
017	James A Moore	1998-1999	5						-	-	-		1			1
018	Matt Bullock	1998-2017	223	80 . 4	1	513	29	3-12	17.69	6.36	16.69		74	24	9	107
019	Howard Jones	1998-2004	34	193 . 1	15	827	45	5-9	18.38	4.28	25.76	2	7			7
020	Kevin	1998	1						-	-	-					0
021	Noel Reilly	1998-2000	3						-	-	-					0
022	Adrian Deans	1998	1						-	-	-					0
023	Lee Davie	1998-2005	14	54	4	163	12	3-15	13.58	3.02	27.00		2			2
024	Leo Beletsky	1999	1						-	-	-					0
025	Mike Thorburn	1999-2001	18	67 . 4	9	304	14	2-17	21.71	4.49	29.00		1			1

	Career Records	Seasons	M	O	M	R	W	Best	Ave	Econ	SR	5wi	ct	st	ro	tot
026	Robert Phillips	1999	3	6	0	35	0	0-15	-	5.83	-		1		1	2
027	James Hoskins	1999-2017	302	1403	110	6493	316	4-15	20.55	4.63	26.64		79	1	20	100
028	Stuart Redfern	1999	1	9	4	12	3	3-12	4.00	1.33	18.00					0
029	Matthew Lloyd	1999	1						-	-	-					0
030	Simon Dickens	1999	2	21 . 4	2	85	9	6-23	9.44	3.92	14.44	1	2		1	3
031	Philip Holt	1999-2000	3	6	0	24	2	1-8	12.00	4.00	18.00					0
032	Clare Norris	1999-2000	15						-	-	-		2			2
033	Michael O'Leary	1999	2						-	-	-		1			1
034	Gus Da Cenha	1999	1	3	0	5	4	3-4	1.25	1.67	4.50					0
035	Tony Mander	1999-2010	68	7 . 5	0	81	3	2-10	27.00	10.34	15.67		11			11
036	Ben Mander	1999-2012	68	142 . 2	3	916	33	4-31	27.76	6.44	25.88		13			13
037	Jess Ball	1999	1						-	-	-					0
038	James Dale	1999	1						-	-	-		1			1
039	Paul Grant	2000	6	2	0	21	0	0-21	-	10.50	-					0
040	Lorcan Kennan	2000	5	1	0	10	0	0-10	-	10.00	-					0
041	James Yarwood	2000	1	4	0	26	2	2-26	13.00	6.50	12.00		1		1	2
042	Greg Le Tocq	2000	12	75 . 4	14	243	18	4-11	13.50	3.21	25.22		2			2
043	Paul Drake	2000-2002	12	26	2	137	5	3-17	27.40	5.27	31.20		3			3
044	Andrew Morley	2000-2010	51	15	0	113	2	1-8	56.50	7.53	45.00		1			1
045	Leo Phillips	2000-2002	16						-	-	-		3			3
046	Adrian Fisher	2000-2011	48	91 . 4	11	468	36	5-15	13.00	5.11	15.28	1	7		1	8
047	Jake Hotson	2000-2017	265	66	3	444	16	5-28	27.75	6.73	24.75	1	38	19	9	66
048	Nick Watney	2000	3	9 . 4	0	53	5	3-8	10.60	5.48	11.60					0
049	Lloyd Mike	2000	1						-	-	-					0
050	Richard Hadfield	2000-2017	48	5	0	33	2	1-10	16.50	6.60	15.00		16		2	18
051	Steve Ray	2000	1						-	-	-					0
052	Steve Merivale	2000	1						-	-	-					0
053	Kate Atkinson	2000	1						-	-	-					0
054	James Smith	2000	1	2	0	13	0	0-13	-	6.50	-					0
055	Steven Walker	2000-2002	4						-	-	-					0
056	Steve Dobner	2001-2017	184	603 . 2	45	2562	125	4-9	20.50	4.25	28.96		40	6	15	61
057	Thornton Smith	2001-2017	232	445	19	2591	127	3-12	20.40	5.82	21.02		57		9	66
058	Mike Rogers	2001	1	3	0	4	0	0-4	-	1.33	-					0
059	James Mander	2001	6	31	4	86	3	2-15	28.67	2.77	62.00		3		1	4
060	Grant Smart	2001	1	1	0	11	0	0-11	-	11.00	-					0
061	Atul	2001	1						-	-	-					0
062	John Greany	2001	1	4	0	30	0	0-30	-	7.50	-					0
063	Matt Baker	2001	1	5	2	23	3	3-23	7.67	4.60	10.00					0
064	Niraj	2001	1	3	0	12	2	2-12	6.00	4.00	9.00					0
065	Dylan Jones	2002-2004	21	108	4	538	21	4-17	25.62	4.98	30.86		2			2
066	Jay	2002	1	7	2	20	1	1-20	20.00	2.86	42.00		1			1
067	Shaki	2002	1	3	0	15	1	1-15	15.00	5.00	18.00					0
068	Ian Harwood	2002	2													0
069	Nigel Sawyer	2002	1						-	-	-					0
070	David Grundy	2002	1	2	1	4	1	1-4	4.00	2.00	12.00					0
071	Nick Hebbes	2003-2017	107	301 . 2	25	1420	66	4-17	21.52	4.71	27.39		33		2	35
072	Martin Westmoreland	2003-2017	258	464 . 3	35	2443	112	4-19	21.81	5.26	24.88		111	2	16	129
073	Steve Hebbes	2003-2008	27	119 . 4	10	547	32	4-7	17.09	4.57	22.44		6		1	7
074	John Harris	2003-2008	28	131	11	644	44	7-5	14.64	4.92	17.86	1	13		2	15
075	Graham Bridges	2003-2004	16						-	-	-		1			1
076	Paul Henley	2003	1						-	-	-					0
077	Ian Howarth	2003-2017	305	662 . 4	44	3385	157	5-5	21.56	5.11	25.32	1	74		21	95
078	Shoaib Ahmed	2003	1	4	0	14	2	2-14	7.00	3.50	12.00					0
079	Sudharkar Selveraj	2003	1	4	0	20	1	1-20	20.00	5.00	24.00		1			1
080	Justin Jackman	2003	1	4	0	18	1	1-18	18.00	4.50	24.00					0
081	Neil Howarth	2003	1	4	0	13	0	0-13	-	3.25	-					0
082	Marco	2003	1						-	-	-					0
083	Michael Horton	2003	1						-	-	-					0
084	Paul Williams	2004	1	7	1	26	0	0-26	-	3.71	-					0
085	Michael Clarke	2004-2009	24	19 . 3	1	137	2	1-9	68.50	7.03	58.50		6			6

	Career Records	Seasons	M	O	M	R	W	Best	Ave	Econ	SR	5wi	ct	st	ro	tot
086	Dan Edwards	2004-2012	123	312 . 3	20	1372	83	4-12	16.53	4.39	22.59		33		7	40
087	Gary Littlechild	2005-2010	30	8	0	24	1	1-6	24.00	3.00	48.00		7	10	4	21
088	Victoria Stone	2005	1	0					-	-	-					0
089	Geoff Carter	2005-2017	108	11	0	99	1	1-25	99.00	9.00	66.00		20	8	15	43
090	Richard Kemp-Harper	2005	1	8	0	40	4	4-40	10.00	5.00	12.00		1			1
091	Steven Arnold	2005	1	4	0	22	0	0-22	-	5.50	-					0
092	Andy Cavanagh	2006	10	2	0	16	0	0-6	-	8.00	-		3		1	4
093	Mike Reeves	2006-2017	226	901 . 5	83	3867	185	5-12	20.90	4.29	29.25	3	73		14	87
094	Steve Parkinson	2006-2016	27	149	25	489	24	4-31	20.38	3.28	37.25		6			6
095	Adrian Small	2006-2008	20	70 . 3	6	371	12	2-23	30.92	5.26	35.25		4			4
096	Dave Shorten	2006-2017	160	720	100	2857	133	4-4	21.48	3.97	32.48		47	1	15	63
097	Petr Benisek	2007	2						-	-	-					0
098	Andrew Darley	2008-2017	46	266	30	986	34	4-20	29.00	3.71	46.94		9		1	10
099	Ian Leggate	2008-2015	72	75 . 1	0	736	24	5-40	30.67	9.79	18.79	1	10		1	11
100	Huw Leggate	2008	1	7	2	17	1	1-17	17.00	2.43	42.00					0
101	Jenner Collins	2008-2011	4	7	0	54	1	1-39	54.00	7.71	42.00		1			1
102	JP Collins	2008-2009	15	70	4	384	20	3-11	19.20	5.49	21.00		7		1	8
103	Andy Washington	2008	1						-	-	-					0
104	Alex Washington	2008	1						-	-	-					0
105	Dave Emerson	2009-2017	168	734 . 4	111	2845	139	5-25	20.47	3.87	31.71	2	37	1	5	43
106	Brad Harsant	2009	2						-	-	-					0
107	James Pearson	2010-2017	147	441 . 5	33	2095	107	5-20	19.58	4.74	24.78	1	44		16	60
108	Ross Maher	2010	1						-	-	-					0
109	Chris Roberts	2010-2017	177	729 . 4	3	3743	122	4-26	30.68	5.13	35.89		34		12	46
110	Paddy Mellor	2010-2017	61	20 . 1	0	180	7	1-7	25.71	8.93	17.29		11		3	14
111	Jack Cox	2010	1						-	-	-					0
112	Gareth Timms	2010-2017	159	633 . 5	26	3336	149	4-17	22.39	5.26	25.52		28		10	38
113	Ted Jordan	2010	1						-	-	-					0
114	Lee Ainsworth	2011-2017	63	141 . 4	16	596	45	4-27	13.24	4.21	18.89		17		2	19
115	Jon Newman-Robson	2011-2017	57	369 . 2	42	1308	64	5-10	20.44	3.54	34.63	2	19		5	24
116	Rob Eaglestone	2011-2012	7	2	0	19	0	0-19	-	9.50	-		1			1
117	Mark Rundle	2011-2017	71	301 . 3	32	1354	51	4-19	26.55	4.49	35.47		18		1	19
118	Ralph Smith	2011	1						-	-	-					0
119	Rob Arkell	2011	1						-	-	-					0
120	Sandra Steinhauer	2011	1						-	-	-					0
121	James Shaw	2011	1	2	0	16	0	0-16	-	8.00	-		1			1
122	Russell Turner	2012-2017	130	35 . 5	0	255	11	2-9	23.18	7.12	19.55		36		3	39
123	Jan Webster	2012-2017	36	63 . 2	1	345	11	2-16	31.36	5.45	34.55		4		1	5
124	Nick Hill	2012-2017	38	20	0	154	7	2-7	22.00	7.70	17.14		6		3	9
125	John Nash	2012	1	2	0	8	0	0-8	-	4.00	-					0
126	Jamie Whiting	2012	1	5	0	28	1	1-28	28.00	5.60	30.00					0
127	Adam Ward	2013	10						-	-	-		5			5
128	Hugo Scott	2013	4						-	-	-					0
129	Steve Lawrence	2013	1	7	1	36	3	3-36	12.00	5.14	14.00		1			1
130	Rahman Aliza	2013	2	7	0	49	2	2-49	24.50	7.00	21.00					0
131	Stuart Ackland	2013	2	11	1	62	0	0-13	-	5.64	-					0
132	Dan Emerson	2013-2015	3	21	3	95	5	2-22	19.00	4.52	25.20					0
133	Matt Reading	2014-2016	14	32 . 5	1	186	6	2-18	31.00	5.66	32.83		1		1	2
134	Quintin Sanders	2014-2015	1	8	1	32	0	0-32	-	4.00	-		1			1
135	Mark Shelley	2014-2015	2	15	2	36	1	1-25	36.00	2.40	90.00					0
136	Sami Mughal	2016	2	4	0	24	0		-	6.00	-					0
137	Graham Wilson	2016	1						-	-	-					0
138	Nick Parnell-Smith	2016	1						-	-	-					0
139	Dave Barlow	2017	1	3	0	26	2	2-26	13.00	8.67	9.00					0
140	Polly Moon	2017	1						-	-	-					0
141	Cornelius Vermaak	2017	7	10 . 2	0	83	2	2-17	41.50	8.03	31.00		1			1
142	Srinivasan Janarthanan	2017	1	3	0	22	1	1-22	22.00	7.33	18.00					0
143	Daniel Shaw	2017	1	2	1	11	0	0-11	-	5.50	-					0
144	Chris Williams	2017	12	14	0	97	1	1-39	97.00	6.93	84.00		5			5
145	Simon Coates	2017	1	5	1	33	0	0-33	-	6.60	-				1	1

A WORD FROM OUR PUBLISHER

An interview with Russ Turner

Ian Howarth and Mike Reeves

SO the back story to this is:

As previously mentioned, Russell Turner is a good guy and generous to a fault. When the idea of a book was first mentioned he immediately offered to put his commercial business on hold and apply his million pound printing press to spitting out a few copies of our vanity project. Later, as the writing neared completion he offered to write a chapter about his time as stand in captain and in particular how his first nine matches ended in defeat.

Conversely, Mike Reeves and Ian Howarth are inconsiderate gits, with an over inflated sense of their own literary abilities. On reading Russell's chapter, they thought it was "overly long, meandering, too full of unnecessary statistics and covering ground already described in previous chapters". It therefore wouldn't be included. Ian phoned Russ to convey all this, with all the subtelty of a train wreck, thus ensuring Mr Turner's evening out with his wife (to watch Roger Daltrey at the Albert Hall) was ruined. Ian then phoned Mike to say that Russ had thrown his toys out the pram, was not talking to them and the publishing was on hold. This was a lie, Russ is in fact bigger than that and took their criticism in good heart. So now Mike hates Ian whilst Russ has every right to hate the pair of them.

In this atmosphere of acrimony, Russ, Mike and Ian agreed to meet to interview Russ and try to tease out the story of his captaincy in a way which wasn't overly long, meandering etc etc, but mainly to take the piss out of those nine consecutive defeats. Here is a record of that interview:

Q1, so Russ, just so we're 100% crystal clear, you are still going to publish the book, right?
(long pause)… yes. Of course.

Q2, good, glad we've got that out the way. Now we've established you can't write about cricket, do those nine consecutive defeats also mean you can't captain a cricket team?
Certainly not, I believe I have captaincy in me and I'm always ready to learn. I'm your go to guy when nobody else will do it.

Q3, what ever possessed, I mean what first inspired you to captain the team?
I was talked into it when Moo suffered one of his catalogue of infamous injuries and Howarth couldn't be arsed to do it. 2013 I think it was.

Q4, of those nine consecutive defeats, which was the one that got away, the one which we (i.e you) should really have won?

Harwell, we lost by a dozen or so runs. We threw that one away and the blame lies solely with Geoff Carter. The ball hit me in the groin when I was 48 not out, and the doddery f_____ triggers me. I was really pissed off and it niggles today.

Q5, of those nine consecutive defeats who would you apportion the blame on most? (i.e who really let you down)?
Definitely Geoff, George, Godfrey godforsaken bloody Carter!

Q6, did your style of captaincy change as defeat followed defeat followed defeat followed defeat followed defeat followed defeat followed defeat followed defeat followed defeat?
No. It inspired me. I know people thought I was clueless and incompetent, and I'd never skippered before, but Gary repeatedly left me in the shit against the strongest teams!

Q7, talking of which, are you irked by our regular skipper, Mr Timms, seemingly unavailable for all our toughest games, preferring instead to spend his time on weddings, stag dos and impromptu holidays?
Gary is an inspirational skipper, but it's a diabolical liberty being able to swerve the games against the toughest opposition because it doesn't do your statistics any good.

Q8, as captain, do you think you could do more for the team? We appreciate you making the effort to regularly make teas, transport the kit bag and collect subs on the day, but are you skimping on your duties?
I can buy a mini-bus and pick everyone up before the game, I can pay everyone's match fees and supply sponsored kit. You f______ serious?

Q9 go on then, tell us what it was like to finally captain a winning team.
Ohhh, Harwell away, twelve months after *that* Geoffrey bloody Carter fiasco. We put up a decent score and things were tight, until Davis holed out to Moo on the deep cow boundary. What I truly remember is Ainsworth's send off "you didn't dance around that f_____ did you?" directed at Mr Khan after the batsman was continuously dancing around his crease and had his stumps rearranged. The elation was unreal on winning, as I fell to my knees I looked up to skies and said "get in you f_____, the drinks are on me!"

Q10, forever the bridesmaid never the bride, d'you think the shadowy MAD Committee will continue to invent ways to prevent you becoming skipper elect? Will Gary ever resign? (i.e every year is his last)
Gary will probably resign, sometime, although I don't think that'll happen until his stats are better than Moo's. I will skipper, probably, but I'd need support what with my work commitments and everything. I'd need a good vice skipper, such as James Pearson, who basically does *all* of Dave Shorten's bidding for not a lot of thanks.

Q11, lastly and of course this is totally subjective so won't appear in the book (*another lie from Mr Howarth*), out of the players who have played under you, who has been the most supportive and who have been the biggest pains in the arse to deal with?
Howarth, Ainsworth and Dobner (the brothers of moan) are constantly whinging, though I try to ignore them . Thorn is Thorn, so it's pointless telling him where to go as he simply stands on the boundary with a fag in his mouth and sometimes a beer. Talking of Howarth, what is it with these ex-skippers? Always second guessing you and mucking about with your field when your back's turned?

Those I like in the ranks are Reeves, as he's ever consistent and knows what needs to be done, Darley and Salad don't need to be managed either. Ditto Matt. I like Pops Williams, I think he's going to be quite a character. I also like Lucan, but when is he ever bloody available?

Q12, lastly lastly lastly, what was your best win?
Astons away, undoubtedly, when Ralph Smith came in at #4. It put pressure on John Shea as opener and put pressure on himself. I was smug as f___ about that win.

We thank you for your time and patience Russ. We promise to edit your responses to the best of our obviously superior literary talents, thus ensuring you can half-boast about being a published author on the same pantheon as ourselves. ■

Selected Index